Teresa Parker

Common Sense

in Child Rearing

COMMON SENSE
IN
CHILD REARING

ERNA WRIGHT

HART PUBLISHING COMPANY, INC.
NEW YORK CITY 10003

Contents

Introduction

You have no doubt picked up this book because you are a parent, or expect to become one soon. So it's too late to debate whether or not to have a child. You have joined the club. You will spend a good part of the rest of your life as teacher, guide, nurse, companion, absolute authority—a symbol of the roots every human being puts down in some way, someplace. In short, a parent.

Loving your child is instinctive; liking him or her is something else again. It presupposes your child is likable— and to turn a demanding, selfish newborn baby into a happy, healthy five-year-old takes a good deal of upbringing. That's what *Common Sense in Child Rearing* is about.

Now, I know this isn't the first book on the subject. A new one comes with every change of fashion, and fashions in raising children change as fast as they do in pop music. Consider the difference between the dogmatic approach to every aspect of a child's routine laid down only thirty-five years ago, and the permissive attitude that is often advocated now. *Common Sense in Child Rearing* is not fashion-conscious. After all, babies are human beings, and don't alter all that much over the years.

Certain basic theories always work, even though they may appear in new forms. True, each individual grows and changes all the time; but the path of change follows certain landmarks. This book—based on my training as a nurse, my experience as a mother, and my long general observation of mankind in miniature—is intended to help parents recognize a child's stages of development, and to help steer them through the maze of advice, good and bad, they will encounter once they find themselves with a son or daughter.

Son or daughter, he or she . . . Can we agree right now that I shall refer to your child as "he"? But even if "he" is a little girl, rest assured it is your child I'm talking about. Most of the time, that is.

Of course, I can't guarantee that all children will behave alike in similar circumstances. They're not puppets, thank heaven, who react in a certain way when we pull certain strings. So every time your infant behaves in a way that does not conform to what my book says, take comfort from a fellow sufferer. I have three children, none of whom did what the pamphlet I was using insisted they'd do. The point is to learn to cope with your own child's nature, and that's what I hope to show you how to do.

Cope—perhaps that word conjures up the wrong image. It sounds rather as if we're viewing parenthood as an ordeal, considering only the crises and tantrums of the infant and the confusions and contradictions of the hormone-bubbling teen-ager.

So let's think about the rewards instead. Now, if you expect to feel a sense of reward right off, perhaps when you come home from the hospital, you are doomed to disappointment. Your sense of the excitement and wonder of being a parent is liable to be clouded by all the things you feel you are so inexpert at, so *bad* at. Then one day you find that something you've done for your baby—you've fed him, you've changed him, you've put him back in his crib, or whatever—has been good for him. He isn't resisting or furiously upset. Quite the contrary; he's quiet, and later on he may even smile at you. This is the first of many rewards to come.

This sense of reward will be yours throughout your relationship with each other, even when the child is somebody's husband or wife. True, the sense of reward tends sometimes to be overshadowed by anxiety, irritation, or fear, and there will be occasions when you will wonder: "God, was it worth it?" But I'm sure that the times when you feel how nice, how fulfilling it is to have a child, will easily outweigh the other times—provided you are a reasonably intelligent parent.

Being an intelligent parent means using your common

sense and your instincts. Being an intelligent parent means being selective about the advice you accept from well-meaning friends or, for that matter, from professional experts like me. And being an intelligent parent means learning to live as a family instead of as just a couple.

Equally, however, your child must learn to live with you. This has perhaps been forgotten by a generation of parents who heard a great deal about the danger of giving children complexes or frustrating them, and as a result have reared offspring who thought the house and the world itself were run exclusively for their benefit.

Every child must learn to fit into a particular household with particular rules and with things particular to it, just as any baby learns to eat the national dishes of the country he happens to be born in. Indian children go from milk straight to curry because curry is all there is. And they seem to do very nicely, thank you. As long as a diet contains vitamins and minerals and protein, it doesn't matter much whether the food is curry, ragout, or steak and onions. That's what I mean about learning to live in a particular environment.

While parents might be willing to reorganize their entire way of life merely to suit the child, sooner or later there'll be someone in the child's life who won't be at all willing, and what a rude shock that will be! For instance, if this reorganization procedure is repeated when the second baby comes, the first child may well be unable to adjust himself to the life style dictated by the newcomer. And most important, if the baby doesn't learn to fit himself into one household, what chance does he have to fit into the world?

We have to be aware all the time that child rearing is

more than just looking after a baby. We are educating a human being, who must eventually know everything we know—plus, we hope, at least a little more. This education means learning how to survive—being aware of the dangers of scissors, electric plugs, saucepan handles, matches . . . It means learning to become socially acceptable—having respect for other people's feelings and property. Finally, it means learning self-discipline. Inevitably, the last process starts by learning Mommy's and Daddy's discipline.

I know it's hard to disappoint your child and say "no," but sometimes you must. I've been told about a child who goes to bed every night with his shoes on—yes, honestly. I gather that once, while being undressed after a tiring day outside, the little boy refused to have his shoes taken off. Instead of ignoring his "Don't!" and calmly removing the shoes anyway, the mother faltered, the child shouted, and lo and behold, this disgraceful habit was begun. Apart from the harm to his feet and the sheets, what about the less apparent harm to the boy's character? Moreover, if his parents couldn't take a stand over such a clear-cut question, in how many other more serious matters does he get his own way?

Please don't get the idea that I regard you as the Big Chief. I don't. You are not the boss, nor is your child the boss. But ultimately, because you are older and wiser, because you have responsibility for him morally and ethically, as well as legally, what you say goes.

Even so, you must be certain that what you say is absolutely reasonable—like, "You do not wear your shoes to bed, they're for the morning when you go out to play again"—and not just a decision you make in a flash of temper, or to please somebody whose pleasure isn't that important—I'm thinking here particularly of a strong-willed Grandma.

Grandmothers often wield unholy power over their grandchildren, insisting this or that is what should be done. Remember, the grandparents had their day with you or your husband. It's your turn now. Be courageous, stick to your own beliefs.

Children have a great sense of justice. If you suddenly change the rules to suit an outsider, they'll know it and feel betrayed.

Generally speaking, your child reacts as you do. Just because he is smaller than you doesn't mean that he's of a different species. He will be hurt by a mechanical "Very nice, dear," when he's telling you about a game he's invented, just as you are by a "Yes, dear," when your spouse hasn't listened to a word you've said. Similarly, your child will be as delighted with a spontaneous hug from you as you will be with a sudden hug from your mate.

Try to treat your child as a person, not as something called a baby. And beware of thinking of him as "my" child. Certainly you gave birth to him, you provide his comforts, you're his lifeline—but all this doesn't make him your property. You're only entrusted with his life until he's fit to take over for himself. The concept of "my" child may suggest to him that you do own him. And it goes both ways: if he's "your" child, then you're "his" mother.

There are many small children—you see them in the street, in restaurants, on airplanes, trains, buses—who really

16

think they do own their mothers. They demand and command constant attention. That's not good for either child or parent. So encourage your child's independence and hold onto your own. Apart from anything else, the day will come—long after this book has immediate application for you—when he will require something other than the mother-child relationship, and you have to prepare him for relationships with his peers.

Talking of independence, I think perhaps it is important to mention that, exciting as it is to be a mother, a woman may tend to forget that motherhood is only a part of her life. A woman should remain a person in her own right, with views and opinions about things other than how to look after a baby. And she also has to remember that she has another role—that of wife.

Many difficulties in marriage, many difficulties in father-child relationships, occur because unconsciously Father resents the fact that he has gained a child but lost a wife. This is why I've always suggested to young expectant parents that social life should not stop once the baby arrives.

Since pregnancy lasts only nine months but rearing the child takes eighteen years, it's vital that you do not abandon your social activities. Presumably you didn't immerse yourself so deeply in your marriage that you were no longer an individual but merely somebody's wife. So in your new maternal role, don't let yourself become merely somebody's mother. Nature may have intended this, but you're not an animal in a wood. Fight the temptation.

Apart from it being better for yourself and your

husband that you should remain Ann or Mary as well as Mother, it's better for the child. Just imagine how dull it would be living with someone who could never be a companion because all she thought about was cooking and laundry and report cards.

This recognition of your right to retain your individuality is one of the good aspects of postwar attitudes toward child rearing. One of the not-so-good aspects is a curious desire to find deep-seated psychological motivations for every response from a child.

I've seen a little girl fall and scrape her knee and shed tears out of all proportion to her pain. Her "modern" parents then psychoanalyzed the situation, and decided that the display of emotion was subconsciously intended to frighten them because she felt they had rejected her last week.

Well, could be . . . But isn't it far more likely that she cried so much because the pain was just a little bit greater than any she'd experienced before, or because, besides having a sore knee, she was tired?

Don't let a happy parent-child relationship become an exercise in psychotherapy. It will just worry you and make the child tense and uncertain. Only when it is obvious that a child is seriously disturbed should a mother be on constant guard, with the guidance of a specialist.

By now you will have gathered that *Common Sense in Child Rearing* is about the How of childhood, rather than the What of childhood. It is not intended to be a factual handbook.

I won't attempt to deal with all the varieties of patent

baby foods, and the advantages of one over another. Nor will I give precise instructions on nursing a child suffering from measles. This kind of information should be obtained from your doctor, or from the numerous pamphlets and books devoted specifically to this sort of information. (Incidentally, as we go along, I may mention specific things—a particular piece of equipment or a particular method of sterilizing. The ones I name are merely examples, and I am not implying that any other brand or method isn't just as good.)

All very well, you say, but I still want to use *Common Sense in Child Rearing* as a reference book. How do I do it? In the first place, there's an alphabetical index at the back; so if you want to find out about moving your child from his crib to a bed, simply look up "crib," and read the appropriate page.

Alternatively, you can see from the contents page that "Cleanliness" is obviously going to talk about washing, bathing, and so on. Moreover, I've organized the chapters chronologically from birth to five years.

You have, let us say, a nine-month-old baby. Every time you attempt to put him on the pot he becomes tense, he screams, he kicks. What are you doing wrong? Well, if you turn to the chapter on toilet training you will find a section on the nine-month-old. Or, if you are having difficulty with breast-feeding, you turn the page to Chapter 1. In fact, why don't you start there right now?

Common Sense

in Child Rearing

1

Feeding

Babies are individuals. Their needs differ. They don't come with identical built-in clocks all ticking away in unison. Feeding by the clock is necessary in a hospital to permit the maternity ward to function, but each baby in that ward would probably prefer a different mealtime.

So as soon as you get your baby home, it will help enormously if you let him more or less determine when to eat—and when to eat should be when he's hungry. This generally does work out to five meals every twenty-four hours, at least in the first three months. Whether some meals come after intervals of three hours and others after seven doesn't matter a bit.

I'm breaking my rule in this chapter, you see, and telling you in handbook fashion what to do, instead of just what to expect. There are far too many conflicting views on feeding babies, and some of these notions are just plain harmful. Since the feeding of a baby forms the basis of his physical and mental growth, it is too important to leave to chance. Here are some common-sense suggestions on what is right for your baby, even though it may not be easiest for you.

Breast-feeding is the best way to give a baby a good start in life, for he absorbs immunities and antibodies from his mother's milk that cannot be put into a formula. Though there are good alternatives, there is no substitute for mother's milk.

But not every woman can breast-feed. Nor does every woman want to breast-feed, for whatever reasons. These women can buy or prepare formulas under their doctors' guidance that will make little difference to the child's development. Store-bought formulas such as Similac or Enfamil, however, are pretty rich for the budget; it's much cheaper to mix one's own.

Many women want to breast-feed but don't produce quite enough milk. In the hospital, they probably got a supplementary bottle to give their babies after breast-feeding. That was fine, since there was somebody else to bring the bottle. But it's not so good at home where, more than likely, a woman must attend to her baby by herself.

Under those circumstances, the supplementary bottle represents a doubled chore. You must breast-feed the traditional ten minutes a breast, and then dash out to the kitchen and mess around with bottles. So, most often, the breast-feeding goes by the board.

If you are a woman who can't breast-feed adequately every time, it's far better to plan alternate feedings. For example, give your baby a leisurely breast-feeding around 2:00 P.M., when just you and the baby are at home, and a bottle feeding at 6:00 P.M., when you're also coping with your husband's dinner. If you feed your baby this way, Similac, Enfamil, and the like are handy time-savers, well worth their extra cost.

When and How to Add Solid Foods

When you should add solid foods depends upon what your baby needs. Some babies require solids when they are as young as three weeks. In a research project in one famous London hospital, babies were fed solid food from birth; although there were no significant improvements in the babies' development, solid food certainly didn't do them any harm.

But most experts advise that a baby be given just milk—breast or formula—until he is obviously no longer satisfied with it. At this time you can add to the baby's milk small quantities of precooked cereal. (To feed solids to a baby, use a *plastic* spoon. Aunt Emily's solid-silver christening spoon may turn black in a sterilizing solution.)

Remember that your baby is accustomed to sucking from a nipple, a mouth action quite different from sliding food off a spoon. So your baby's first attempts at eating from a spoon are likely to be clumsy, and he may well resist the innovation. Persist gently. If you put a little food on his lower lip so he'll lick it off, he may find the experience so pleasant that he will be willing to take the food from a spoon.

On the other hand, it may be the food he distrusts. Don't force the baby to eat if he refuses; just give him his milk and try again at the next feeding. If he still resists solid food, go a couple of days longer before trying again. It may be a matter of getting used to a new taste.

Don't add sugar or any other sweetening to cereal. The cereal is flavored to a baby's palate. Anyway, I'm against white cane or beet sugar for babies. About 5 percent of American babies—and much higher percentages in other countries, such as Greece and India—can't digest sugar and it aggravates colic. Other sweeteners will develop tastes that guarantee whopping dental bills in later years.

In the first three months, cereal is all that need be added to the diets of most babies. So, unless the doctor suggests you provide baby with a wider variety of mixed semisolids, leave it at that. The doctor will also advise you when to begin administering vitamin C and cod-liver oil, or a substitute.

Fruit Juices: Fresh vs. Canned

The baby's main source of vitamin C, of course, will be fruit juices. However, most commercially packed juices contain lots of sugar. It's pretty silly to keep sugar out of your baby's cereal, and then give it to him in juices. And if you do, he may refuse to take cereal or milk that *doesn't* contain sugar.

So buy juice oranges and squeeze half an orange a day for him. (Do not save the other half for the next day—a cut orange quickly loses the potency of its vitamins.) This method is more trouble and a little more expensive than spooning out the canned or bottled stuff, but if you care about your child's health—and especially about his dental health and your dental bills—take my advice.

Cutting Out the Sugar

But suppose you are reading this book when your child is already a few months old. You may be muttering: "Heavens, I have given him sugar, sugar, sugar all the time. I had better stop." Well, you can . . . but you'll have a very unhappy child on your hands for several weeks, and in the end you may well give in out of desperation. So it might be wiser simply to start reducing the quantity little by little. You could also stop using white sugar and substitute honey or brown sugar as a sweetener, or even glucose.

The Social Side of Feeding

One of the most important things for a baby to learn is how to relate to the people around him. In his first few months,

27

the greatest opportunity for forming relationships comes when he is being fed.

Now, when a baby is being breast-fed, he inevitably will be cuddled. Unfortunately, this is not necessarily true when he's bottle-fed. One doesn't have to hold him close to get the milk into his mouth; actually, one doesn't have to hold him at all. It is all too possible to leave the baby lying in his crib with the bottle propped up so that the nipple is in his mouth.

But you should know that every year a large number of babies under the age of six months choke to death while being fed this way. Almost as important as the physical danger is the fact that the baby is being denied the human contact he desperately needs.

Imagine putting your husband's dinner in front of him every evening and then going off to do something else. Wouldn't he soon begin to suspect your love for him? In our society we use the occasion of eating to strengthen relationships. That's why we go out to dinner with friends. That's why your husband takes you to dinner—I hope—on your birthday; he's using the meal to let you know he's fond of you.

You can't tell your baby that you love him in words he understands, but you can tell him by physical contact. After all, he's had the most intimate contact for nine months; to expect him now, abruptly, to do without close maternal contact is unfair.

Killing the Germs

You have to have sterilizing equipment. One young mother told me that she religiously rinsed her baby's bottles, cereal bowl, and the like with boiling water in the belief that this killed bacteria. A word to all such innocents: rinsing cleans but doesn't sterilize.

Of course, you must wash the baby's bottles and utensils in soap and water, or a good commercial solution. But you must also sterilize in boiling water: bottles, nipples, their covers, your tongs, the plastic spoons used for mixing milk and for the feeding itself, and the measuring cup in which the milk or formula is mixed. Boil them for at least twenty minutes in a container with a tight-fitting lid.

After boiling, drain the water, replace the lid, and let the contents cool sufficiently so that you can remove the tongs. With the tongs lift out bottles, nipples, etc., as you need to use them. And if you drop a nipple on the floor, don't pick it up and use it simply because it's just been sterilized. Get another sterilized nipple.

As your baby passes the six-month mark, there is less and less need to sterilize anything, except the bottle and nipple. Milk harbors bacteria harmful to an infant and gastroenteritis can be fatal. For his cups, spoons, bowls, and plates, normal dishwashing will do, but wash them first, not in greasy water after the pots and pans. Then let them dry on a rack instead of wiping them with a dish towel—even the cleanest-looking of dish towels isn't likely to be clean enough for Baby.

If you have to go out for the day, take enough sterile bottles with you to give your baby as many feedings as he will need. While you're on the go, you won't find time or place to sterilize a bottle or nipple.

Home Cooking vs. Packaged Foods

Some babies are quite happy on just cereal and milk until they're four or five months old. They gain weight satisfactorily; they're bright; they're contented; they sleep well. Until this state of affairs alters or until your doctor or clinic instructs you to do so, you don't have to introduce any new foods. But the majority of babies, as they pass three months, start to require additional protein and vitamins. This is the time to teach them that not every food tastes like milk.

I'm sure you know that many baby foods—dinners, desserts, and even snacks—come in cans, jars, and boxes. This is indeed a convenient method of feeding a baby, and I know you have a lot to do besides cooking up a spoonful of carrots. But to my mind, these foods should be used only by people who have no choice—people who are traveling, or on vacation, or have to leave the baby with a sitter.

For the average mother, fresh lightly cooked foods that she herself makes into purée are infinitely preferable. For instance, there's a ready-made lamb stew with vegetables on the market. Well, Baby should have lamb stew with vegetables, but he's better off with your version of it. For example, you can control how little (if any) flour your own stew contains. Flour is starch, too much starch means a fat baby, and a fat baby, it has been proved, often grows into an overweight child and perhaps an obese adult.

So use your own stock. The butcher will have bones you can stew. Add puréed vegetables to the stock, along with the juice from the meat you roast for your Sunday dinner.

You can also include in Baby's diet: the yolk of a soft-boiled egg (the white is often indigestible for babies in their first nine months of life); steamed fish, flaked (use a fresh fillet like cod rather than something like flounder, which has many small bones you may not see); or grated cheese, which when melted in milk and poured over a vegetable purée, makes an excellent substitute for meat protein.

Much the same applies for desserts: give your baby puréed lightly cooked apple; puréed orange; mashed pear or banana; and such fruits as plums and berries. Purées are easily prepared in a blender.

When Baby Wants to Help

During the period when baby is between three and six months old, he will increasingly want to join in the feeding process. After all, you can't expect him to lie there as he did when he was new, just sucking at the nipple with eyes blissfully closed. Now he will at least reach out for your hand.

If that's all he does, and he remains fairly passive, conveniently opening his mouth at regular intervals like a young bird, good. But more likely his little hand will get in the way, so give it something to do. Many babies are satisfied if you give them a spare spoon to wave while you're using the working spoon.

Your baby may not be so easily put off. He may insist on gripping your spoon regardless, and you will need both your hands to get that banana into his mouth instead of on his chin, on you, and on the floor. If you have one of these determined little tough guys, sit him in his high chair or prop him up in a corner of the couch for his food, cuddling him on your lap only for his milk. Still, he'll probably still attempt to grab your hand, your face, the spoon.

All right—it takes longer, it's messier, you may have to wear a large apron. But even though your baby's "help" makes life a little more difficult, try not to discourage it. Unless today is a day when you've a train to catch, or Great-aunt Gladys is coming and you want the baby spotless, let him begin to learn to hold something in his hand and lead it to his mouth. One day soon he'll be able to do it firmly, and that will be an exciting step forward.

2

Weaning

If you are still breast-feeding by the time your baby is six months old, I believe that for a variety of reasons you should now start weaning him on pasteurized milk. He's had all the vital antibodies from you that he needs, and to carry on breast-feeding much longer is sheer indulgence—either of your baby or of yourself. So start replacing the 10:00 A.M. breast-feeding with a bottle. After about a week—when he's happily adjusted to that change—replace a second feeding. If he's still having a 10:00 P.M. feeding, choose that one to replace; if not, make it the 6:00 P.M. feeding.

After another week, replace the 6:00 A.M. breast-feeding with a bottle. And a week later still, replace the 2:00

P.M. feeding. This should complete the changeover for most babies. But for those who are feeding five times a day, it will take an additional week to cut out the 6:00 P.M. breast-feeding.

It sounds easy, doesn't it? Fortunately, for most mothers it is. But for some it can be uncomfortable, and for a few, painful, because for a while the breasts will continue to produce milk that is no longer being drawn off. If you're one of the unlucky ones, see your doctor.

To prepare bottled milk for your baby, measure the right amount into his sterilized bottle and stand the bottle in a pot of very hot water to warm it to the temperature he likes. Test a few drops of milk on the inside of your wrist to make sure it's not too hot, and don't let any drip on Baby.

Babies vary in length of time they need a bottle. If your child is content with the bottle and makes no attempt even to reach for a cup, let him keep his bottle. Many babies have grown into happy, healthy human beings despite the fact that at eighteen months they were still drinking from a bottle with a nipple. Remember, sucking is a powerful stimulus that babies need for varying lengths of time. Don't try to make your child grow up before he's ready.

On the subject of drinking, never give your child a glass which could be dangerous for him. And don't give him a china coffee mug either; that could be dangerous for your china. The best solution is to give him a plastic cup, or a plastic mug that has a lid with holes—the lid prevents spilling and the mug is a sort of halfway house between a bottle and a cup. Six- and seven-month-olds often take very happily to these mugs with lids, but don't be surprised if your child proves an exception. None of my three children liked them either, but readily accepted ordinary mugs.

Introducing Three Meals a Day

Here the process is mainly one of cutting down on milk and increasing the amount of solids. Eventually milk becomes a drink rather than the baby's main food. The baby's digestion is getting stronger all the time. Try giving him a little of whatever you're eating unless the food is highly seasoned; he'll probably welcome the variety. Naturally, mince or purée it to suit him.

Once milk has been de-emphasized, you should aim for three meals a day—a recognizable breakfast, lunch, and dinner routine. Water or fruit juice should be served with his midday meal, and milk as a midmorning or last-thing-at-night drink. Incidentally, even though your baby may be taking his milk from a cup happily at other feedings, you may find he'll want a bottle before settling down for the night. He finds the sensation of sucking soothing. Don't deprive him of it without his consent.

And how does he indicate his consent? By not bothering to suck properly through the nipple for about three days in succession, but accepting the same milk from a cup. Then you know he's concluded that the pleasure he gets from his bottle isn't worth the effort.

By the end of this period, Baby's milk intake should be down to between a pint and a pint and a half per day (ask your pediatrician for guidance). Snack feeding may well have been cut out altogether.

By this time, too, your baby will have made regular attempts to reach for the spoon. But don't give him a spoon and insist that he learn to feed himself. If he wants to, splendid. By now, anyway, he will probably hold a piece of zwieback or toast and suck or chew at it. This is good for his teeth and gums, and good for his learning how to get food from hand to mouth. Certainly he'll never conquer this complex skill if it's only your sure hand that makes the journey.

Warning Signals

During the whole weaning period, be sure your child's digestive system is dealing with all the new substances you are feeding him. Watch his stools. If he becomes constipated or his bowel movements become loose, eliminate whatever food you have introduced in the last twenty-four hours. Wait several months before offering it again.

The other signal to look out for is a rash—not necessarily all over his body. If one develops, go to your doctor immediately. *You* don't know, but *he* does, whether this is measles or simply an allergy to something your child has eaten.

3

Cooking for Baby

Once your child has several of his upper and lower teeth, including molars—generally after the age of sixteen months —it is not necessary to mince his food. If you cut it up into small pieces, he can eat what the family eats. That means, most probably, that you will have to cook twice a day—for your child at lunchtime and for yourself and your husband in the evening.

The Ingredients

Children do not need complicated recipes. What is important about their meals is what's in them. Steaming a small

37

portion of fish over one potato in an aluminum colander doesn't take long. Cooked green vegetables have no special virtue for a child. A salad of lettuce, young spinach, or any raw vegetables the child likes—grated carrot, chopped celery, tomato, cucumber—will do just as well.

If you are cooking a casserole for dinner, you can prepare it in the morning so that it will be ready by lunch. Then you can give your child a little of it and reheat the rest for dinner—it won't do the casserole any harm. On the contrary, its flavor will be improved.

If you aren't making a casserole and you had fish yesterday, cook three to six ounces of ground stewing beef, roasting veal, or neck of lamb. They'll take no more than twenty minutes' work and, though they're inexpensive cuts of meat, they are as nourishing as filet mignon. Put the meat in the oven, and cook it slowly in gravy in a covered heatproof dish.

However, not all meat for young children has to be cooked slowly. If you're serving a lamb chop, veal cutlet, or liver, fry or grill it as you would your own. But afterward cut the meat up very small, of course.

Then make gravy for it by mixing a minute amount of beef broth or gravy with the water in which you have cooked vegetables. Boil this up with the meat juices that have run out into the pan (first draining off the fat). Gravy is a must for toddlers; they nearly all like their food very moist.

If today's menu includes a small potato, one carrot, and some spinach, you don't have to have three pots all working at once. One will do. Babies eat their food mixed up, anyway, so it doesn't matter if the spinach flavors the potato.

Boil a well-scrubbed potato in its jacket (the nutritional goodness sits mainly just under the skin). When it's half cooked, add the spinach and chopped carrot. Thus, all will be ready at the same time, but the greens won't be mushy.

Put the spinach and carrot on your child's dish while you peel the potato, then return the potato to its pot to be mashed in butter. The hot potato, the hot gravy, and the hot meat are sufficient to warm up the whole meal to your child's taste.

On weekends there's no problem. Baby can share your roast or chicken.

Your child's supper should also contain other protein. You can give him macaroni and cheese on a day when he ate boiled egg for breakfast. And why not baked beans or a little fish occasionally? Fish doesn't have to be fresh or frozen; it can be canned tuna or sardines. At dinner and breakfast, use bread and butter, toast, or zweiback as an addition to his meal, not as the main course.

Dessert and Treats

I am opposed to pudding for dessert. Pudding means starch. A piece of cheese and fresh fruit—an apple, or an orange with the seeds and membranes removed—needs no cooking and is much better for him.

Teach your child to drink water when he's thirsty,

instead of soda pop. Make ice cream an occasional treat rather than a daily habit. Never let him get the idea that he can raid the pantry for cookies whenever he feels like it. Bad eating habits lead to obesity and tooth decay.

4

Teaching Baby How to Eat

At about this time, when your child has grown a few teeth, he will probably learn in earnest to feed himself. When he's acquired this skill, he'll become fiercely independent and resent any help. Once he can eat on his own without spreading food all over himself, the table, and anything else nearby, it's a good idea for him to have his meals with the family.

This is the time to put your baby in a high chair. When he's in it, you can see what he's doing (no mean advantage, this) and, more important, he is at the right height to see you. Though he sits at his own table, at least this is pushed up against the family table; thus mealtime becomes a social occasion in which he participates.

Household routines differ, of course, and if your husband comes home from work after seven you can't very well keep a one-year-old up so that he can eat with his parents. But he can have breakfast and lunch with you, and perhaps at weekends he can eat with you both. A child, after all, is a small person, not somebody from a different planet, and the more he can share a family activity as important as dining, the better.

At this stage there is no question of introducing formal table manners. To expect him to handle a knife and fork would be ridiculous. But you can reasonably expect him to put his food into his mouth as tidily as he is able. Teach him in a friendly but firm manner. Until he can do it well, help him. And when you have guests, don't subject them to watching a child dribbling poached egg down his chin. Feed the child beforehand.

When He's Eighteen Months Old

From eighteen months upward, the child will increasingly eat what and when the adults eat. This shift in diet is especially important if you already have a three-year-old in addition to the new baby. It may be tricky to fit in the main meal for the older child, the two o'clock feeding for the baby, and a bite of lunch for yourself. This makes for three quite different sessions at the stove—and your meal and the three-year-old's ideally should be ready at the same time, so that you can sit down together.

Well, there is no reason why your eighteen-month-old child can't have soup and scrambled egg, or a cheese dish and fruit, with you for lunch. His dinner meal should then be taken around 5:30 (if you and your husband usually eat that early, the baby can eat with both of you).

There's no problem about taking your child straight to bed after eating. In fact, Nature intended us to curl up in our caves immediately after our burnt bearsteak. Think of your pets—they sleep after a meal. Think of Grandpa after Christmas dinner—doesn't he doze in the armchair?

But bear in mind that your child shouldn't bathe within an hour of a big meal. You might consider switching his bathtime to morning.

Once your child has all his teeth, you need no longer cut up his food finely; just cut it into bite-size pieces. As his appetite grows, increase the protein in his diet (meat, eggs, cheese, and so on) far more than the vegetables and starch.

Soon you will no longer need to mix his food but can serve it instead in separate little mounds—a smaller version, in fact, of your own plate. Children, too, need their food to look appetizing.

When your child can cope with such a meal all on his own (with an adult doing no more than the cutting up beforehand), it is time to transfer him from his high chair to a bulky cushion at the dining table.

43

Tomato Sauce Three Times a Day

All children, however placid they are about eating what's put in front of them, do develop periodic dislikes for certain foods. If you accept these whims calmly, however, the antipathy tends to transfer to something else—perhaps from greens to mushrooms, and then from mushrooms to scrambled eggs; and in the end the child may like scrambled eggs but dislike bacon. These phases of disliking a food—for its color, its texture, or its taste—are not serious and will probably pass.

Nor should you worry about your child's taste for a certain food almost to the exclusion of everything else. It might be tomato sauce or corn flakes. Indulge his passion, but don't overindulge it. Tomato sauce three times a day will become tiresome even to its most dedicated admirer.

For most children, highly spiced foods should be avoided. But there are some children who have a positive addiction to such things as mustard, pickles, and strongly flavored cheeses. So to some extent be guided by your child's likes and dislikes.

The Sweet Tooth

While on the subject of passions, let's talk about the curse of the '70s—candy and sweets in general. A generation or two

44

ago, sweets were rationed to youngsters by vigilant mothers. For many of today's children, they are available on demand. There are four reasons why this is bad.

First of all, for the sake of their teeth. Second, for your budget. Third, eating sweets between meals ruins the appetite, and your child won't manage to finish the meat and vegetables he truly needs. And last, but certainly not least, providing sweets on demand is bad for his character. We know we can't have everything we want any time we want it, nor would we be happier if we could. This applies to your child, too. He must learn that he cannot pop a chocolate in his mouth whenever he feels like it, and he ought to be able to pass a candy store without getting a lollipop or an ice-cream cone.

Of course, this doesn't mean that he must *never* eat sweets. That's a little too Victorian. But help him to regard sweets as a treat rather than as part of his diet.

When I pass out candies myself, I tend to overdo it, but that's not so bad as you might think. A dentist I know assures me that the harmful deposit left by a half-pound of candy is only a trifle worse than that left by a couple of candies. It's the continual, steady eating that does the real harm.

Actually, handing out excesses of candy has its advantages. It works on the same principle as serving tomato sauce three times a day for a week. The child feels ever so slightly fed up with candy, and it may be two or three days before he wants more.

In my own family, each of my three children had his own candy jar which I kept in a cupboard. They could ask for their jars whenever they wanted candy—but they knew that once their jar was empty, it would stay empty until I felt like buying more. As a result, they rationed themselves, and also got used to doing without candy for relatively long periods.

What about those goodies you can't control—the ones friends give your child and the ones he buys with his own pocket money? In the second category, inflation helps cut down consumption. Presumably you're not going to give your under-five-year-old more than a dime a week for spending money, and that won't buy him a killer dose—not when he's also got to save for marbles and another model car. Anyway, he may sometimes need to buy candy for social reasons—you know, to win friends and influence other small people.

As for the candies he's given, your concern should be proportionate to how often it's likely to happen. If Grandma is going to indulge him every single Sunday, stop her. But if you spend a once-a-year afternoon with the wife of your husband's boss and her spoiled child is given a daily bowl of M&M's, ignore the sugar intake today for the sake of your husband's career.

"I Hate Spinach"

Candy or no, there may come a time when your child suddenly hates the lunch you've cooked for him. Perhaps he's just not hungry today. You needn't force a child to finish food he obviously doesn't want. But neither should he leave his liver and bacon and eat his ice cream instead.

Often a child will indicate he doesn't want vegetables, for instance, the moment he sees them on his plate. In my family, we had a system for dealing with that problem—the instant a child said, "I don't like that," we said, "Fine, all the more for us," and portioned it out among the rest of the family. The resistant child would usually keep his portion the next time. Most children go through temporary phases of "I hate fish," or "I hate spinach," but eventually their preferences will not prevent them from eating whatever is served.

Now, suppose you or your husband do hate some food, yet you reckon that your child ought to eat it because it's good for him. He'll know you dislike it, even if he is only a few months old. A baby is particularly sensitive to attitudes, however much you think you are disguising them. So don't be surprised if he resists you as firmly as you probably resisted the person who tried to make you eat spinach. It is better to avoid giving a child food that you do not care to eat.

Sometimes, too, you may give your child food you or your husband have never tried. Though you know it is good for him, try it yourself anyway. Your child will probably learn to like it, and perhaps you and your husband will be persuaded to eat it, as well.

When to Start on Table Manners

Before we end this chapter, we ought to talk a little about table manners. If you're having a feeding problem—however temporary—it is obviously not a logical time to interrupt your child with a "Not like that, dear." It would be adding insult to injury to expect him to hold his cup elegantly when he's just rejected the milk in the cup. The food itself is the vital thing. Sophisticated table manners can be successfully instilled later.

Nonetheless, the earlier that manners are taught, the more automatic they become. Once your child is about two years old, gently but firmly start to correct him. Any habit can be acquired only by repetition. Be prepared to say the same thing over and over again: to put down his knife and fork; whether to eat with only a spoon or with a spoon and fork, one in either hand; why he shouldn't blow bubbles into his milk.

Introduce your child to the standards you expect in your family. Table manners vary from household to household just as they vary from country to country, so teach him behavior that you feel comfortable with, not some textbook etiquette.

Be warned: if most of the time you allow your child to eat as he pleases—with his hands, or putting food on his head—you cannot suddenly expect perfect table manners from him when you are visiting friends. Learning table manners is a slow process.

Stories at Mealtime

I don't recommend making a meal the occasion for a story, the kind that continues so long as the child eats and stops when he stops. Nor should you indulge in any of the variations on "Let's see who can eat this faster, you or your brother."

Such activities make a problem out of mealtimes. They are not necessary. Parents may start these practices in an attempt to distract a child who is temporarily going through a difficult phase with his eating—probably while he's adjusting to new flavors. They think that if they can only get the food into their child while he's thinking about something else, they're helping him. They're not. On a deep level they are convincing him that he must have some compensation for swallowing this unpleasant substance called food.

EATING SHOULD BE A PLEASURE. Regard it as such, and sooner or later your child will, too.

5

Cleanliness

A clean baby is a delight and a dirty one is, well—something quite different. I have seen in my time a lot of babies who, to my mind—and nose—were not so clean as they should have been. Yet keeping Baby clean from top to bottom is no great problem even in his first fifteen months. Let's begin with his bath.

Bathing

Even if you have been taught in school or in a baby-care clinic how to bathe a baby, you are likely to approach your first baby's first bath with trepidation. You will feel clumsy, and horrible thoughts will besiege you the first few times you fill the tub: "Suppose he slips out of my hands and drowns." "Maybe the water will be too hot and I'll scald him." And so on.

First of all, it's highly unlikely that he will slither out of your grasp but if he does, just pick him up again, quickly and calmly. That's what you're there for, along with testing the water's temperature with your elbow—not with your hand, which isn't sensitive enough.

It isn't necessary to spend a lot of money on a baby's bathtub, by the way, because he will soon outgrow it. The cheapest plastic tub will do for the first few months. After that, a bath in the family tub will be much more fun for him. And there will be more room for splashing and kicking and sliding around, with Mother's help. Most babies come to look forward to bath time as a play period.

Bathing your baby every day is not essential. Of course, you may prefer to give him the daily ducking, but that's a question of his pleasure and your conscience rather than one of hygiene. The point is that you don't need to feel guilty because you didn't get around to bathing him to-day. Washing his face and his bottom twice a day is really enough to keep him clean on days when you skip the bath.

After he can sit up by himself, you will no doubt introduce all the usual bath toys that family and friends provide. You and your husband might as well face the fact that for several years your bathtub will be cluttered by ducks, fish, boats, and weird underwater craft. Harbor them in a plastic net shopping bag, hanging on the wall, to keep them out from underfoot when you take your own bath.

Encourage Independence

The time will come when your baby is no longer a baby but a small child who will try to help wash himself. I know you can do it more efficiently and faster without his assistance, but your child needs to do things for himself as soon as he can.

Some children wouldn't dream of touching a wash cloth or a piece of soap until they're two-and-a-half. Often this is true of an only child who doesn't spend much time with other children. Children who go to nursery school generally want to wash themselves earlier than do those who stay home with Mother. So do children with older brothers or sisters; as a rule children are quicker to imitate other children than they are to imitate adults. (Perhaps the hardest task is teaching the oldest child how to be independent. The others will learn by watching him.)

But at any time after your baby is fifteen months old, he may want to hold the soap when you wash his hands and face. Next he'll try to wash his own face with the sponge or wash cloth, which will, of course, drip and soak his clothing. Nevertheless, these attempts should not be discouraged. It is only when the child reaches the point where he wants to wash himself that you can begin to teach him that a wash cloth can be squeezed so that it isn't dripping wet.

Once you've got his interest, teach him how to wash his neck and ears. And if he's been playing in a sandbox or out in the yard, introduce him to a soft nail brush for his fingernails. In any case, hand-washing before all meals, and after using the toilet, is a must. Keep a spare wash cloth and towel in the kitchen for him.

Learning to Brush His Teeth

By this time, too, you should have started cleaning your child's teeth with a soft toothbrush. At first you may use just water, but he'll soon need toothpaste. A flavored fluoride toothpaste made for children may not have any medicinal advantage over its adult equivalent, but your child will prefer its taste—and a willingness to have his teeth brushed is half the battle.

Show him the right way to brush, which is not to push the toothbrush from side to side but up and down. Bear in mind that when you brush his teeth, he can't see what you're doing in his mouth, only feel it. So his first attempts to brush his own teeth are bound to be clumsy. You may find that you will make better progress if at first you clean his teeth properly, and then give him the toothbrush to do them again. Never let him fiddle with his teeth first and then correct him. That's crushing for a youngster.

Runny Nose

Nothing makes your child less acceptable socially than a constant snivel and a wet stream moving like a glacier toward his upper lip. Until your child is approximately two-and-a-half to three years old, wiping his nose is something you will have to do.

Now, there is nothing more unhygienic than a cotton handkerchief. It is a germ-carrier, and only prolongs a cold. Use disposable tissues. Or if tissues are too expensive for your budget, perhaps you have an old worn sheet that you can cut up into handkerchief-size pieces. But dispose of them immediately after use—don't wash them to use again.

From about the age of two-and-a-half, a child should be taught to blow his nose. This is a muscular skill and, strange as it may seem, it isn't something he will discover for himself. (In communities where no one bothers to teach children to become socially acceptable, seven-, eight-, and nine-year-olds run around with runny noses.) The act of blowing is difficult to describe, so the following game may be a help to you.

Take an ordinary bowl, fill it with water, and float a small feather—perhaps one from a pillow. Next, put your hand firmly over your mouth and attempt to move the feather by blowing at it through your nose. This action is exactly the one you use when you blow your nose. Invite the child to watch. (Don't do this as a punishment for having a runny nose, but as a game. And, naturally, choose a time when neither of you has a cold.)

He'll think the game fun and want to join in. Perhaps you will need to put your hand over his mouth until he gets the idea that the only way you can play is by not allowing any air to pass out through the mouth. As soon as your child learns how to move the feather, he has learned to blow his nose.

"Why Do I Have to Wash?"

Sooner or later your child will ask you, "But why do I have to wash?" You could say: "Because it will keep you healthy." But that sounds awfully dull. To a healthy person, there's nothing so boring as health; only sick people are obsessed with it. And I am assuming your child is well.

I'd take the attitude that we wash because it's nice to be clean. It is infinitely preferable to associate cleanliness with a pleasant sensation than to associate dirt with nastiness. Dirt is not necessarily nasty. It depends on what you're doing.

Sand may be dirty, but if your child is playing in a sandbox, then sand is nice. If he mixes it with food, or gets it on the rugs, it becomes undesirable.

If you are gardening and your hands are working in soil, dirt is not nasty; on the contrary, it is pleasant. But it becomes something different if you go into the kitchen and begin to cook without washing your hands. So press home the association of cleanliness with niceness, and get away from the idea that "It's nasty to be dirty."

6

Toilet Training

Every so often I hear a young mother, while changing a diaper, complain to her baby about the mess he has made and the nuisance of cleaning him up. The baby may not understand the words, but he gets the idea. It would be far better for both Baby and Mother if she took a positive approach and said: "Now, isn't it nice to be all clean again?"

Your success in toilet training your child will depend on your attitude toward what is, after all, a normal bodily function. The less emphasis on excretion as something nasty, the better.

Many adults imagine that children are born with an instinctive revulsion to their own excreta. This is not so. On the contrary, many psychiatrists believe that, for babies, producing excreta is making a gift to Mother. If Mother's response to the gift is revulsion, the child will sense it. At best, he will be puzzled; at worst, hurt.

So please try to control your acquired attitude that excretion is vile. You will be benefiting your child's emotional health, and you may eventually feel less revolted yourself.

Diapers: Cloth vs. Disposables

Now, on the question of baby's underpinnings . . . As you know, there are many different kinds of diapers on the market. There are the conventional square cloth diapers; there are shaped diapers—a little more expensive, but useful because they fit more snugly—and there are the disposables.

The disposables certainly have their value, particularly when traveling, but I wouldn't really recommend them for day-to-day use. First of all, I believe they are not so comfortable as cloth. Secondly, those that I have seen are not so absorbent, and mothers who use them all the time have to change them twice as often.

"Ah," you argue, "but you're not the one who has to wash the soiled diapers." True, but the toil and trouble of diaper washing as our mothers knew them are happily things of the past.

Most places have diaper services, but if you consider them too expensive, or do not have one in your town, you need not despair. It is no longer necessary to boil diapers to kill the germs they inevitably collect. Supermarket and grocery store shelves are laden with solutions designed to sterilize diapers and remove the stains. (Most of them are also ideal for your baby's sheets, bibs, cotton suits, or dresses.)

If diapers are still stained after you have used one of the sterilizing solutions, wash them in pure soap flakes. A word of warning here: harsh detergents and biodegradable washing powders may produce diaper rash. Don't ever use them for diapers and baby clothes, however well they work on things like dish towels, pillowcases, and your husband's shirts.

If you have a back yard, it's a good idea to put all your baby's washing out for a while and let the fresh air blow through it. The fresh air not only makes diapers softer and sweeter-smelling, but also combats germs. If you don't have a back yard or a suitable rooftop, I recommend that occasionally, especially on wet days, you toss the baby's wash into a tumble drier (at home or in the local laundromat).

It is an old-fashioned idea that diapers have to be ironed—they don't. With all the new drip-dry materials, the task of coping with the rest of baby's laundry is also considerably reduced.

By the way, you can avoid the worst soiling on diapers by using a disposable liner (available at any drugstore or baby shop) inside the cloth diaper. Then, when you next change your baby, you simply flush the soiled liner down the toilet, and the cloth diaper will still be clean.

I like the new "one-way-traffic" kind—the ones in which wet passes through and cannot get back again, so the surface next to the baby's skin remains dry. These liners are ideal for those nights when you don't have regular opportunities for changing your baby, for they keep him free from diaper rash and irritation.

Diaper Rash

Do sponge Baby with warm water *every* time you change him, even when the diaper has not been soiled; although the skin looks clean, the salts from urine cling to the skin surface and can cause as much irritation as excreta can. Dry him thoroughly. You don't have to use towels; tissues or absorbent cotton will do.

Pat on baby powder, or perhaps a little baby cream (I recommend Johnson's) if you suspect the beginnings of any soreness. Watch out for this particularly when your baby is teething, because teething often causes upsets. Here as always, prevention is better than cure. But there are babies who have especially sensitive skins, and in the case of persistent irritation, you should consult your pediatrician.

When to Abandon Diapers

This brings us to the question of how long you should continue to use diapers. That depends on your child, not on you, but you can help him to give up diapers when he is ready. Psychiatric research of the last few decades has indicated that early toilet training is undesirable. It strains the baby's nervous system, because it makes him anxious about something that he can't control.

Although I have never encountered a mother who insisted on early toilet training and who punished her child if he didn't succeed, a mother's pleasure at seeing her three- or four-month-old on the pot brought its own stresses. Your baby wants to please you, but he simply can't.

I happen to be one of those mothers who attempted early toilet training with my first child. My elder daughter, now a mother herself, used to tell people when she was in her teens that she was "her mother's experiment." She was right, and the experiment was "successful," too. I could proudly announce that by the time my daughter was fourteen months old, she needed diapers only at night. But she still had tensions about going to the bathroom.

With my second and third children I was less ambitious, and they in turn were far more relaxed.

How to Begin Toilet Training

Somewhere between a year and eighteen months—only you can decide when your own child is ready—introduce the pot. This works better if it is done as a game at first, rather than as something very serious and very needful of success. So at first use the pot without relation to its real purpose.

I remember that my baby and I carried ours from here to there; we bowled it from one end of the room to the other; we wore it as a hat. Only gradually did the pot go to its rightful place beside the toilet, where it then stayed. Children are conservative by nature, and like to learn where things belong. They don't like having things that they're accustomed to seeing in one place be suddenly in another.

Then, finally, came the day when I took the child to the bathroom, removed his diaper, and sat him on the pot. Of course the child had no idea what to do. So I made his sitting on the pot coincide with my own visit to the bathroom, and by imitation the child discovered slowly what was supposed to happen on this pot. If the very idea of this embarrasses you, do overcome it for your child's sake. There's no reason for embarrassment.

Naturally I praised the child when he first succeeded, and on a number of occasions afterward, but I feel strongly that excessive praise is bad. A "good boy" or "good girl" is enough. In the course of repeating this over and over, making no comment when the diaper I took off was wet—which meant that it was too late for him to succeed in the pot—he quickly and willingly began to cooperate.

My children also learned what the pot was called. Actually, it is not unusual for children who are trained in this way to include the word "pot" among their earliest words. They will say "pot" when they want to go to the bathroom, and you will drop everything and dash.

Though some children learn this much earlier, you can expect your child to ask for the pot before he excretes into his diaper by about the age of two. In fact, the more calmly you can treat toilet training, the easier the process will be. And if you avoid anxiety or excessive praise, it will never occur to your child to use his pot as a weapon—performing obediently when you're in favor, using his diaper when he's annoyed with you.

We should consider what exactly it is that we are trying to teach a child when we commence toilet training. We are helping him to adjust to some things quite new to him:

1. To the fact that his bowel movements or urine are waste, and are removed as soon as he has passed them.

2. To the realization that this process is apparently linked with Mother's approval.

3. To the idea that approval is nice; and that he can create the event which brings approval.

He will find out *incidentally* how to control his bladder and bowels.

When you first show your child the "how and what" of a pot, it is easier to get some results in the pot if you plan your attempt for a time when you know he usually has a bowel movement, such as about half an hour after breakfast. Also, it's worth having a try each time you change his diaper—especially when he's just awakened in the morning or after his nap.

Now, I appreciate that you can go through this drill for weeks on end with a nineteen-month-old, regularly sitting him on his pot while you use the toilet, and he'll not once get the message. If you think you could catch him if the pot were in the room where he was playing, fair enough. Then temporarily—and only while you're alone together—take the pot to him (or in summer even out into the yard).

Once he is "clean" (I hate that term) and can be counted on to urinate into his pot at least twice a day, stop using diapers in the daytime and put him in trainer pants instead. With these, the whole toilet-training rigamarole is easier.

Some Tips on Timing

Potty chairs are not potty training; neither is leaving a child on the pot for half an hour or longer. There is then no connection between the purpose of sitting on the pot and the result, which, when you consider the time factor, is virtually inevitable. In this case the child is not performing the act of excretion deliberately but is merely undergoing an endurance test.

I've heard some mothers complain that their children have emptied their pots on the floor or against the walls. I suspect such children were victims of an-hour-on-the-pot, and this was their protest. Who can blame them? Make it five minutes at the very most.

For some children even brief trips to the bathroom are a bore. A small toy that he can play with while sitting on the pot may make your child more willing, even eager, to go there. So you could keep such a toy alongside his pot—but do not, of course, bring your child a full-size doll house or a big toy truck.

If your child resists your effort to seat him on the pot—if he cries, stiffens, clings to you—IT'S TOO SOON. Your child isn't stupid; if you put his bare bottom on this hard plastic thing, he'll understand vaguely what you want of him and realize that it's something he can't provide. That distresses him. So put the pot away for a month and then try again.

Night Training

I know some little girls who between the ages of two and three learned simultaneously how to manage without diapers at night as well as in the day. But they are not many, and boys very often need diapers at night for much, much longer. It is not unusual for four- or five-year-old boys to need diapers at night for complete safety.

For night training, all you do is put the child on the pot at his bedtime and again at your own bedtime. Perhaps the diaper doesn't stay dry in-between, but sit him on the pot regardless to establish a habit. There is no point in sitting him on the pot every two hours during the night. I have known some mothers to do this, but the only results were a tired child and a tired mother.

An important aspect of the way a child learns control is that he is able to maintain that control for longer and longer periods. In the daytime it's not unusual for a child to need to go to the pot every two hours, but to encourage him to do this at night is really working against toilet training.

There may be a short period when your child succeeds in going through the night but wakes at six o'clock positively bursting. Until he can pull his pajama trousers down or she can lift her nightie and sit on the pot, I'm afraid you will have to get up and help. But take heart; it doesn't last long.

One factor in night training is that some children continue to need diapers as long as they are given diapers. But there comes a time in every mother's life when she wants to put her child in pajamas without a diaper—and she should let him know that he hasn't any diaper, and risk wet pajamas by morning.

I hardly need add that the mattress should have a waterproof cover, so that if the child does wet, little harm is done—only pajamas and a sheet to wash. Next night, maybe you'll be luckier.

Your child may need an incentive to help him stay dry. Perhaps some new pajamas that he himself chooses could be sufficient. Or maybe a change of environment—a stay with a favorite relative—may do the trick.

Bed Wetting

But the important thing is that if your child is normally happy during the daytime—if he plays and doesn't show such symptoms of anxiety as sucking his fingers compulsively for hours—the fact that he is still wet at three, four, or even five years old does not mean that he will remain a bed-wetter the rest of his life. If you're particularly concerned, mention it to your doctor; but ten to one, he will only repeat what I've said. Moreover, even if you do have a persistent bed-wetter, he will probably be cured suddenly, even by the most unexpected means.

When my son was nine years old, he had a friend of the same age who was a persistent bed-wetter. Well, we went on a vacation trip to Belgium, and while in Brussels we saw the famous statue of Mannikinpis—the little boy who eternally squirts water into a fountain. The urinating statue so fascinated my son that in a nearby souvenir shop he asked me to buy him one of the little replicas. "I want to give it to my friend," he told me. "It'll help him." Heaven knows how Nicholas knew it, but his friend has not wet his bed from the day he received his Mannikinpis!

What to Call It

We all know many words—none of which is particularly nice—that describe urination or defecation. I personally don't think that any of them are required. There is no reason for a child to tell you what he has done or what he is about to do. To say that he is doing No. 1 or No. 2, or any of the other words for this, is really not necessary; and your child will use such words only if you do.

Why not teach him simply to say: "Potty, Mommy" or "I want to go to potty," or even just "pot." This is not prudery on my part, but rather that our language doesn't have suitable words for a child to use. Besides, we as adults don't hold long conversations about the act; if we say anything, we merely say we're going to the bathroom—we don't go into lengthy descriptions of what we're going to do there!

Now, I admit that in spite of the fact that *you* haven't taught your child any such words, he may well pick one up when he plays with other children. Hard luck. Console yourself that he won't use the word very frequently if you don't use it at home.

From Pot to Toilet

This transition occurs gradually, and to some extent is related to your child's height. For a little boy to learn how to urinate standing up, for instance—and particularly how to do it into the toilet bowl rather than into his pot—he has to be tall enough to reach over the bowl comfortably, or able to cope with a footstool. By the way, you'll probably have to call in your husband here; this is a lesson for a man to teach.

For a little girl, you can buy a child's toilet seat that fits over the toilet bowl and teach her to sit on it rather than on a pot. You then no longer have the bother of emptying a pot, and it makes the transition to the toilet far simpler. But for the sake of guests, don't leave the child's toilet seat in place permanently.

Perhaps in conclusion I should say that although I am apparently permissive about toilet training, in that I don't expect a baby under a year even to attempt it, this doesn't mean that it's unimportant. There is a definite value in teaching your child to use first the pot and then the toilet, instead of the diaper—or worse, running about without a diaper.

I have actually seen this in certain "progressive" homes and I've been assured by the parents that it was one way of allowing the child complete freedom and avoiding repression. To my mind, it is also a way of not fulfilling one's duty as a parent, because it is up to parents to teach their child to fit into society, and society expects its members to use the toilet, not the lawn or the patio or the living-room floor. So we have a responsibility here—a responsibility that, with enough love and patience, we can easily carry out.

7

Father's Role

If you have just given birth to your first child, it may not have occurred to you yet that what had been a relationship between two people has now become a family. Not only are you now a mother as well as a wife, but you are as new to this family unit as is your baby.

Your husband's role is just as important as yours. A father who feels that his job has been accomplished because you now have what you always wanted—a baby—is likely to feel excluded from the intense relationship that will develop between you and your child.

No father is ever so emotionally and biologically involved with his children as a mother; he cannot be. But his need and desire to do what is useful and healthful, and to make the child happy, give your child the sense of security that only two parents can provide. And it is of deep emotional value to your husband as well.

Handy or Ham-Fisted?

Of course, the degree to which fathers are willing to assist in the practical upbringing of a child, particularly in the first three months, is variable. Some men take naturally to feeding the baby, bathing him, changing his diapers and generally acting as your other half when you are busy. Many a man is proud to take his heir out in the baby carriage while his wife is getting the dinner.

But a father doesn't love his child any less if, because of his upbringing, he just can't bring himself to help out that way. The more you bully your husband, the more you insist on having him do the things other women's husbands do, the more resentful and resistant he will be. You can only persuade gently—and appreciate however little or much he does.

Perhaps he would prefer doing something about the dinner while you deal with the baby. Thought about that? Perhaps he genuinely feels a little ham-fisted, fears he might hurt the baby. Men often hesitate about plunging in and playing things by ear, while a woman will say: "Well, I'll make a stab at it. I don't know if I'm much good at it, but

I'll try." In areas that have for centuries been the field of women, men tend to be wary—not all men, but many.

And Baby Makes a Triangle

Remember that the first-time father especially may resent the time you now have to spend with the baby, time you once spent with him. He's relating to you far more in your role as mother and much less in your role as wife. He misses your constant companionship and he feels a bit put out.

That is understandable and quite different from the almost sexual jealousy some men feel toward their child and wife. If you notice that your husband is at all disturbed when you are breast-feeding, take the baby into another room. I know it's contrary to that idealized picture of togetherness you had of the three of you, but it's just too bad. If your husband doesn't like seeing you breast-feed, it's unlikely you can reform him. Don't fight about it; just quietly remove the source of the agitation.

A baby's attitude to his father depends largely on how well he knows him. Babies don't automatically love their mothers, either. They will love those with whom they have contact—and this means physical contact, too. You may be planning all sorts of glorious things for his future, but your baby cannot know he's loved unless he's cuddled, talked to, played with, and his needs attended to. If he doesn't feel loved, he cannot learn to love in return.

71

Just the Two of Them

So if Father is to be loved, if he is to be anything more than the man who brings home the money, he should spend time with his baby. By that I mean from the day the baby comes home from the hospital. He should talk to the baby, play with him, hold him.

Perhaps the best way to encourage your husband to form this active relationship with his new baby is not to stand over him giving directions on how to do whatever it is he is doing. Even though he may be doing it badly, even though he's not doing it the way you were taught to do it in the hospital, go into another room. Leave these two members of the family—your family—alone to get to know one another. Your baby will suffer a far greater wound from having a stranger for a father than he ever will from having a diaper pin prick his behind.

And the other "don't," the important "don't," is not to use Father as the Big Bad Wolf—ever. No matter how irritable your baby is being, to say—even in fun—"You wait till Daddy comes home; he'll deal with you," is creating a nasty concept that he may later on accept subconsciously. So beware.

It is interesting and very touching to watch the different relationship that develops between a father and son and a father and daughter. With his son, he is a pal. With his daughter he is tender and protective.

There is an element of unconscious sexual attraction between father and daughter, just as there is between mother and son. Nothing to get worked up about; it isn't abnormal or wrong. I mention it only because, once you are aware of this attraction, it explains so much. It explains why your own father described your perfectly presentable boyfriend as "a long-haired jerk," and why mother-in-law problems exist. Yes, it is not for nothing that little girls can often get from Father whatever their hearts desire, and that for centuries mothers have been known to ruin their sons with their spoiling.

8

Spacing the Babies

Some babies of course have older brothers and sisters. Since women have been able in recent years to plan their families fairly accurately, a tradition has grown up of the "two-year gap." In other words, the second baby is conceived when the first child is fifteen months. However, I seriously question the value of having children with an age difference of only two years.

During my "Preparation for Motherhood" classes, I was always stressing the importance of not lifting heavy things off the floor, especially without first bending the knees and stooping down slowly. And my mothers protested that they *lived* with heavy objects who continually, and often suddenly, needed to be lifted off the floor—in other words, their eighteen-month-old toddlers!

Apart from the very real threat to her back, a pregnant woman should not be coping with the relentless physical work involved in bringing up a child under two-and-a-half. Once a child is past that age, he may well be exhausting but at least he'll play for an hour while his mother rests on the sofa; he doesn't have to have diapers changed and clothes washed on a day when she's not feeling well.

The Question of Companionship

Then, of course, there are the jealousy problems that may arise when the new baby brother or sister is brought home. A two-year-old is still something of a baby himself. He'll probably still wear diapers at night, he'll still require a lot of help with feeding, he'll still need to be dressed. So he may well feel he's too little to be "replaced," and he will regard with hostility and suspicion the picture of Mommy holding someone else.

A three-year-old, on the other hand, actively wants to be independent; moreover, he appreciates to some degree the advantages of having a sister or brother. He may even nag you to have a baby like Aunt Peggy's.

Yes, you argue, but children three or four years apart are not companions for each other. This is true. But let's be logical about how long that companionship lasts when the gap is smaller. If the children are of opposite sexes, I give it

75

four years at most. I know many brothers and sisters who are more adversaries than friends. All is far happier if they don't see too much of each other during the daylight hours and have their own playmates.

And what about the advantage of getting the "baby period" of your life over with quickly? Well, suppose you have three children, each two years apart. From the beginning of your first pregnancy till your last child's third birthday takes nearly eight years—eight years of milk, diapers, pots, and squalling. Suppose you married in your early twenties and started your family soon afterward—those eight years are your youth.

I quite realize that if you have those same three children at spaces of three-and-a-half years, it takes eleven years—even longer—but at least between each child you and your husband have had a year's break from pregnancy and babies.

Personally I found this vastly preferable. You may not. I'm just asking you not to rush into this two-year thing without due consideration of these factors.

How Big a Family?

Talking of the size of your family, I would say that it is certainly beneficial to have more than one child. The only child is often a lonely child. He doesn't learn about the rough and tumble of everyday living as naturally as he should because he is surrounded by considerate adults.

Thus, when he starts school, it comes as a bit of a shock to him to discover that he has to defend himself against attack. And, of course—owing to the fact that you have much more time—it is far easier, far more tempting, to overindulge an only child. So if it is medically and practically possible, it would be better to have a larger family.

How much larger is for you and your husband to decide. But I would warn you that to be a good mother to more than four children requires positive dedication and a very special sort of marriage; moreover, providing clothes, meals, outings, footballs, tuition, and a hundred-and-one other essential things for six or so children costs an awful lot of money.

9

Jealous Older Children

People attempt to prepare older children for the arrival of the new baby in various ways. I think most fail because they don't appreciate well enough the role of a child in the family.

For example, there's the favorite dodge of telling the child that a new baby is coming for *him*. In fact, I have been informed by little boys and girls of three and four that *they* were having a baby sister or brother. All works splendidly until the baby is actually born. Then there's trouble. The older child very soon realizes that this new property of his isn't a toy with which he can do whatever he wants. Mother and Father won't allow it.

He will also find that his new toy is passive, and it needs things that the owner, for whom the baby was brought, cannot provide. It needs to be fed, for instance, and the owner can't do this—at least, not without considerable adult assistance. It doesn't seem to want to play the games brother or sister may want to play. And it doesn't make the sort of responses a three- or four-year-old or even a two-year-old expects from a playmate. Thus I feel it is much, much better to explain to an older child that the new baby is coming to *join the family*.

So, you think, the child won't be disappointed, but he'll still be jealous . . . Think about this coolly and logically. He will only be jealous if he fears you don't love him as much. And if he has good reason to think that, then you—not he—are the one who needs the psychiatrist. Parents who watch for "jealousy symptoms" tend to get them. On the other hand, a young mother I met recently had never heard about "difficulties with an older child" and therefore didn't expect any when her baby arrived. She has not experienced a moment's trouble in that area.

The Hello Gift

I can honestly say that my own children never expressed overt hostility or jealousy toward the new baby. The only thing I ever did to sweeten the bitter pill of "Well, there is another person here now" is that I had my last baby bring a "hello gift" for his brother and sister. Such a gift doesn't

79

have to be expensive, but it must be bought and correctly labeled in advance, and presented to the older child when he is introduced to the new member of the family.

There is an army of parents who have always done this, only the gift is specifically a doll—"your new baby, dear, like Mommy's new baby." I don't really go along with that because, as you know, I am opposed to "Mommy's new baby" in the first place. He's the family's baby and belongs to no one. If the toy of your toddler's dreams is a teddy bear or a doll, then fine. But the present may just as well be something quite different, like a new game or a baseball bat or a football. Make it whatever your child wants.

In the case of my own second daughter, Merle, who happened to like babies, when her brother came we did give her a glove puppet in the shape of a baby. She did everything she could with this puppet. She couldn't bathe it, because that would have been traumatic for the puppet, but she did breast-feed it. (She was annoyed because the baby never seemed to be taking enough, she told me.) She also kicked it and threw it, and it lost its hands several times in the first week it arrived.

The puppet became a sort of combination of baby, doll, and football. Whether or not she worked out her "unconscious aggressions" on it, I don't know and don't really care. The important thing is, she didn't show any hostility toward her new brother.

The Child Who Won't Adjust

Now, it's just possible that you'll do everything I recommend and your older child—because of his nature, or because of his unusual dependence on you—will still be seriously jealous. He may try to hurt the baby. Stop this for his own sake as much as the baby's (preferably with a tactful "Stroke him gently" rather than "LOOK OUT FOR HIS EYES!"). If he succeeds in bashing little sister with his toy truck, he'll only hate himself in addition to the rest of the world, and the bash won't have removed the baby from his home.

Alternatively, he may try to be a baby again himself—wanting a bottle or refusing to talk. Indulge him if you have to. Just be sure he knows you love him just as much as you ever did, and the mood will soon pass.

But, as I say, the odds are that he'll accept the new member of the family as philosophically, perhaps even as proudly, as you and your husband do. A child won't inevitably be jealous simply because he has to share you with another small person.

A Few More Hours in the Day

Now, what about your *time*—those hours that were once exclusively his? Well, when a woman is caring for her second baby, she is much more expert at such practical

81

things as changing diapers and deciding what her child should wear on a rainy day. Thus she will spend less time on the purely physical care of the second baby than she did on her first.

So you will have that much more time to use, and often you can tend to both your children at the same time—guessing, let's say, the older one's favorite color while you purée the new baby's dinner. On certain occasions the baby may not get picked up when he wants to be, because you're playing with Stephen. On the other hand, Stephen will have to accept that you can't play just now because you're bathing the baby.

Of course, Stephen may like to help with the bathing. But don't count on it. The extent to which I'd advise you to encourage an older child to help with the new baby depends on the personality of the child. Some children love to help; others are just not interested.

Also, there are times when it is not desirable to have the older child present. For instance, while feeding the baby you ought to concentrate your attention on him, not divide it by being Mommy and teacher to your toddler at the same moment. The older child can occupy himself with his toys while you are attending to the baby.

Anyway, wanting to help with the baby is likely to be a sometime thing. It will soon become an awful bore to the child who is given such somber daily duties as holding the soap dish and fetching clean diapers.

By and large, don't worry too much about divided loyalties. I think you will find your day falls quite naturally into times when you can be with both children. And I hope there will still be periods—probably the evenings—for you to be a wife. Not to mention the odd moment to be yourself—to play badminton, to visit a girl friend, or to stand on your head if you like.

Yes. I mean it. All mothers have to learn that they can be many things to many people almost at the same time, and that they can divide the time they thought they didn't have even further.

The Advantage of Coming Second

From the baby's point of view, the advantages of not being the first child outweigh the disadvantages. As we mentioned in the chapter on Cleanliness, second, third, and fourth children learn physical skills such as holding a cup and using the toilet at an earlier age than a first baby, because they make a tremendous effort to be grown-up, like the older child. Later on, they won't resist going to nursery school or kindergarten because this seems a sort of achievement: "I go to school, too."

The games of older brothers and sisters are fascinating for a baby or toddler to watch. Mind you, see that he doesn't interfere with the pleasures of the older child. Don't assume that because he is sixteen months and his older brother and sister are three, they can play together.

The three-year-old has games that the younger child doesn't understand. He has made a house with his bricks, for example, and the toddler knocks it down simply because he doesn't know what else to do. So there is a lot to be said for keeping them in separate game areas—in other words, occupying them independently.

When Your Children Fight

When your children are between three and five years, they will probably play together reasonably happily. Of course, they'll fight. All young creatures fight in the course of play, and punishment in such cases really must be held to an absolute minimum.

I always said "Until they draw blood I'll keep away," and it's probably a good rule. Although one child might punch another, as long as neither feels that he can gain parental attention by being the victim, little damage is done. It's necessary for a child to learn sooner or later that life can be mighty unfair, and that this is something he has to sort out for himself.

While I would not encourage the tattletale, you may have a child who needs to be listened to so that he can pour out his grievances. That doesn't mean you have to go into action about them.

Of course, sometimes you have to intervene and be judge. For instance, a particular toy is wanted by two children at the same time, and you feel it isn't right that the bigger one should always win, nor that the smaller one should always be indulged.

84

Try taking the toy away altogether. The bone of contention is then removed, and they both hate you, but at least they no longer hate one another. A common enemy is a great bond.

10

Where to Keep Baby

While we're talking about the baby as a new member of the family, we might consider where in the house he should live. And since he spends a lot of his first six months asleep, let's begin with where to put the crib. May I make an earnest plea that, whenever possible, no baby should sleep in the same room as his parents?

There are several reasons for this. One of them is the fact that a mother is liable to be anxious and to want "to just have a look at him" all the time—or, worse, to lean over and pick him up. This can be lethal, because Mother is tired when she cuddles Baby, and she is likely to lie down on her bed and fall asleep. Babies have been suffocated that way.

Even if your baby's crib is at the other end of the bedroom, you will be very conscious of his breathing. Young babies do snuffle and grunt and make all sorts of noises in their sleep. It will disturb you, and ultimately you will disturb the baby. Anxiety is transmitted to a baby without words.

You must always remember that a baby can almost read our minds regardless of what we do with our faces and our voices. He has to know. Purely on biological terms, he cannot be exposed to an environment in which he is totally unable to receive communication; therefore, as I said earlier, he is ultrasensitive to the emotions of others.

For precisely this reason he would be aware of the sexual relationship between his parents, and this is to his disadvantage. Having the baby nearby is also, of course, not conducive to a free flow of intimacy between husband and wife.

So if you do have a room to spare, put the baby in it. Believe me, he's tougher than he looks. He is not going to die before the dawn just because he's alone in there. Equally, he should be within "hearing" reach—just in case. So if you yourselves sleep in the west wing of a stately home, don't put your baby in the east wing.

Incidentally, it's perfectly all right for him to sleep in a room with his older brothers and sisters. Most toddlers sleep very deeply and a baby who wakes up during the night— provided he's not allowed to lie there and cry for two hours—will generally not disturb them.

How Long Should He Be Allowed to Cry?

Babies should not be allowed to cry unattended for two hours. The theory that if you lift a baby once, he will expect to be lifted continually during the night, is old-fashioned and harmful. A baby who needs food or drink, or just comfort, during the night should have it. If this is correctly handled—firmly, not overindulgently—almost certainly within the first three months your baby will outgrow the need to be lifted and will then sleep for something like eight hours.

At that point, of course, there's no chance of him waking his brothers and sisters at 2:00 A.M. Moreover, when he does wake up in the early morning, they provide him with companionship.

The baby under six months, however, is going to be hungry, and all the companionship in the world can't compensate for milk. So even though it's only six o'clock on a Sunday morning, if the baby's fretting I would strongly recommend that you get up and feed and change him. Then you can go back to bed with a clear conscience. Any experienced mother will tell you that this is vastly preferable to listening to his whimpers become cries, and lying in your bed hoping he will drop off to sleep again—which he almost never does.

If the baby's older brothers and sisters are early risers, and you like to stay abed, you have a problem. You could try putting them to bed later at night so that they might sleep longer. If this doesn't work, I'm afraid that you'll just have to get up early, too. It's one of the prices you pay for the many satisfactions of being a parent.

If an older child has to be moved out of the crib to make room for the new baby, move him before the baby actually needs the crib. It is better to present the move to the older child as a promotion, certainly not as a sign of being thrown out to make room for the newcomer.

It's a good idea to tell a toddler of two-and-a-half or three that he has now been graduated to a bed like the other adults in the family, and then leave the crib empty for two months or so before moving the baby into it. To take a toddler out of his crib because the new baby needs it and to move him suddenly into a bed is liable to cause considerable resentment, and who can blame him? I wouldn't take kindly to being turned out of my bed for someone else. Would you?

From Crib to Bed

When the time comes to make the move, don't fuss. Your toddler will not hurt himself by falling out of bed. There are no magic magnetic bonds that keep *us* in bed, simply the subconscious knowledge that there's nothing but space on our left or right. It works the same for children.

Occasionally, they do fall out, which is why it's not a bad idea to have a rug for them to land on. But they seldom really hurt themselves. If you're worried, though—so much so that you have to pop upstairs every half-hour to check that he's still tucked in—put two chair backs at the head end of the bed.

I learned the hard way that it's no good to decide that "at two-and-a-half I shall put him in a bed." Children vary as much in this as they do in anything else. For instance, if he has learned to use a pot on his own, why can't he get himself out of his bed to do so? And if he can get himself out, then it's far safer to be a hop from the ground than a jump.

In the case of my own youngest, he learned to "escape" long before I was aware of it. Each afternoon I put Nicholas in his crib for his mid-day rest, and ten minutes later I'd find him curled up on the floor. After a week of this, I began to suspect I was suffering hallucinations. Then came the day of the mighty thump, followed by loud screams. Nicholas had missed his footing on the crib rail and fallen, my four-year-old blithely informed me.

I got the message. Nicholas went into a bed the very next day.

Daytime Habitats

Now let's consider where to put the baby—and here we are speaking of the infant, probably under the age of eight months—during the day.

Whenever possible, wheel his carriage into your back yard or onto your front lawn. Sleeping out of doors is healthy and even the youngest baby enjoys it. But the old idea of putting him out in all kinds of weather because it will make him hardy has fortunately been abandoned. It is downright dangerous for him to be outside on damp days or when the temperature drops toward freezing. But on all other occasions the fresh air will do him good.

If you live in an apartment, you can put his carriage near a wide-open window for most of the day. He will get just as much air. The open window, one or more stories up, is strictly for the new baby, though; once he is at all mobile, you will no longer be able to do this, of course. After the first few weeks, a daily trip to the park or its equivalent will do both of you a lot of good.

Even the youngest babies get bored. This does not mean that you need to entertain the baby all day by making cooing noises or waving colored rattles in his face. It is infinitely preferable for you to organize his daily routine so that he is wherever the rest of the family happens to be.

If his older brothers and sisters are, for instance, doing their homework, his stroller can be wheeled into the room where they're working. The normal noises of two or three lively children are, to him, a stimulus. A word thrown in his direction, an occasional wave or smile, will be enough to keep your baby happy, amused, and interested.

If there are no older children, let him be where you are—in the bedroom you're cleaning, in the living room while you are knitting, in the kitchen, if possible, while you are preparing meals.

"But doesn't he need to be able to sleep sometimes?" you are no doubt wondering. Of course he does. But don't worry about keeping him in an absolutely silent environment. It's not particularly good for him. The sort of house where you ring the front-door bell and somebody rushes to the door whispering, "Ssh, baby . . ." is a house that will eventually have an anxious oversensitive child.

Routine household noises—talking, the humming of a vacuum cleaner, the whirr of a washing machine, water running—will soon cease to worry the baby. He will accept them as normal and enjoy them as evidence that people are around. Sudden loud noises close to his ear may rouse and irritate him. So latch a banging door and suggest to your visiting nephew that right beside the crib isn't the perfect place to toot his new trumpet.

The sound of music, though, is important to babies. They're not discriminating—any old music will do. But a radio in the background will entertain your child and help to develop his sense of rhythm and his love of music.

After three months, when he will be awake longer during the day, you'll probably find that he no longer wants to lie down all the time. So a playpen will be useful. He will enjoy it because he will be able to see all around him and to figure out where the household noises come from.

Bedtime

So much for the days. What about the nights? Your child's bedtime depends on whether he's had a nap in the afternoon. If a four-month-old sleeps soundly from 3:30 to

5:15, wakes and has his supper, and at 6:00 you tuck him back into his crib, he is likely to protest loudly, for he certainly won't be sleepy. He would probably be much happier lying on a rug watching you and your husband eat and then going to bed at 7:00.

Much the same applies to a two-year-old. If he has an hour's sleep in the afternoon, 6:00 is probably too early a bedtime for him. I'm not saying he can't be trained at this age to go to sleep at that hour, but he will probably wake at a disagreeably early hour of the morning.

Some four- and five-year-olds are still perky and bright at 8:00 P.M. or later, others are droopy and cross long before. Make bedtime suit the requirements of your own child, bearing in mind that he should have an opportunity for something like eleven or twelve hours' sleep.

I do think, however, that all children under the age of five should be in bed by eight o'clock—not because there is anything magic about this hour, but because a later bedtime cuts down the amount of time Father and Mother have together as husband and wife—to entertain friends, to sit and talk, to read or just to watch television. Even if the television keeps your child quiet and content, this is the period of the day that should be reserved for your husband and yourself.

We adults know that there is all the difference in the world between a nap on the sofa in our clothes, and going up to bed at night after changing into a nightgown or pajamas. Well, I believe that even a tiny baby can sense the same psychological difference. Nighttime is not a time for Baby to be among the family and all its activity; it is a time

93

for silence and deep sleep. It helps if he changes his clothes—out of his stretch suit and into a bathrobe.

The older child will obviously be changing into pajamas and going off to his room. But if you've one of the sudden droopers—you know, one minute he's playing Indian and the next, just as you've started on your steak, he sinks down on the floor—it might help if he's bathed and changed early in the evening. This way a brief visit to the toilet and a washing of hands are all that's required before you can get back to having your dinner in peace.

11

Growth

"Hasn't he grown?" say relatives and visitors maddeningly, peering down at your child. It's inane, since the one thing we can be sure about is that the normal child is developing physically all the time. The rate of this development, however, will vary from child to child.

You have probably seen lots of booklets and pamphlets which say your child will do certain things at certain ages. For instance, you may have read that a child will smile at Mother for the first time when he's six weeks old, or will attempt to crawl between six and eight months. More children wind up as exceptions than as rules. Timetables did not describe any of my three babies' growth, and these guides may, I fear, frustrate you, too.

I know lots of babies who smiled long before they were six weeks old. I also know poor unhappy babies from institutionalized environments who didn't smile for several months. I know lots of children whose first teeth appeared somewhere between four and six months—which is earlier than the so-called norm—and I know lots of children whose teething started much later.

Is My Child Normal?

The danger in these fixed milestones is that parents tend to worry if their child seems to be "late" in walking or crawling or teething or whatever. They begin to fear that their child is retarded. But how, you ask, will you know for certain that your child is normal if I steadfastly refuse to give you any yardstick by which to measure him?

By observation. If you observe your child and note that he makes definite responses to certain stimuli, you have nothing to worry about. If you suspect that he is not responding adequately, or that he no longer makes responses he once made regularly, do not lie in bed worrying about it and do not surreptitiously compare him with every other child you know of the same age. Discuss it with your doctor.

Even if you write to me, I couldn't possibly help because I've never seen your child. Your doctor has this advantage and—should he have to confirm your fears—is in a position to recommend suitable treatment. But it is far more likely that he will tell you to stop worrying.

Let me reassure you that you will know instinctively whether your child is responding normally to the stimuli around him. Let's say your ten-month-old rears up on his forearms and knees with ease but never tries to crawl. If you're saying as you watch, calmly and happily, "Come on, silly, you can reach your rabbit if you really want to," your attitude is the proper one to take. You are aware that there's nothing wrong with his spine, that he'll crawl when he's good and ready.

If, on the other hand, when a door bangs loudly or you drop a tin tray and your child of over three months makes no response at all, you will naturally become anxious and desperately start manufacturing all sorts of sudden loud noises in the hope that he'll respond to one of them.

This is indeed the kind of situation that justifies serious concern, and you should, of course, consult your doctor to see whether there is something wrong with your baby's hearing. Similarly, if he fails to follow the movements of a brightly colored rattle with his eyes and you realize that he has never really focused on anything, seek advice from your physician.

Keeping Up with the Joneses

Even when mothers know that their child is not retarded, they still compare him with other children, and worry about his "failure" to stand or boast about his "success" in walking. Listening to them, I fear that in this modern age women have developed a new status symbol—the child's accomplishments.

I appreciate that children are going to be a constant topic of conversation, especially if you live where there are a lot of young parents. And it's awfully tempting to throw in, seemingly casually, a "Judy can feed herself now," when you know full well that *her child* can't. It's a wonderful means of paying back all sorts of old scores—like her lawn having flourished when yours turned brown. Conversely, it's hard not to feel a bit ashamed when your child can't do any of the brilliant things being done by her child and all the other children around of similar age.

Similar age . . . let's examine that phrase. A month isn't very much of an age difference when you're in your twenties, but it's a huge gap in the first years of life. So to expect your five-month-old to do the things that the neighbor's six-month-old is doing strikes me as very foolish.

But, you whisper, your child is the elder and *still behind!* Does it really matter? I hope our children are not out to win prizes as prodigies to bolster our pride. And don't hesitate to tell your smug neighbor so if she persists.

The reasons I'm so against this comparing of babies are that (1) it causes unnecessary worry for you and your child, and (2) that it's the wrong kind of competitiveness. You should be helping your child to grow at his own pace, not within a statistical norm. It's cruel to your child to continually prod him beyond his current capabilities, just because you want to keep up with someone else.

Before you acquire this habit, consider the disastrous effects it can have later. You have no doubt heard parents say to their child, "Why couldn't you have made the football team [or the top of the class in math]? Johnny next door did . . ."

The one place where a child should be able to feel that he's accepted as himself is his home. If his own parents compare him unfavorably to others, his sense of security will be undermined. This is equally true of the toddler trying to walk and of the baby who still can't quite roll over on his own. And remember, your attitude can be sensed by your child, and can therefore be just as harmful as your comments.

Since you should help your child to develop at his own pace, we had better discuss how you can best do this. First of all, how do you know whether you're helping him to do something he is striving to achieve, or pushing him into something he isn't ready for?

That's quite simple. Whenever you see your child trying to do something, help him to find out how to do it. But don't suddenly decide because it's a fine Tuesday that "today my child is going to learn to sit up"—and sit him bolt upright, and then be disappointed when he falls over.

For example, suppose you notice that your child is constantly attempting to raise his head, perhaps in order to see something that has attracted his attention. Give him support behind his back to take the strain away.

An excellent way to teach him to sit up is to have him lie on his back on something soft, like the mattress of his crib. Then let him grasp your index fingers with each hand, while simultaneously you grip his wrists to give him additional security, and pull. You'll soon find that *he* will pull, using your hands like parallel bars on which to raise himself. And later, when he is ready, this exercise will assist him to sit up on his own.

Self-Taught Lessons

Of course, you may have a child who resents interference— a do-it-yourselfer. Say, when he's four months old he tries to roll over but is hampered by his far leg; you push it up for him, and he goes red in the face, clenches his fists, and shouts. Seems he doesn't want your help. All right, retreat and leave him to get on with it on his own.

Learning does not necessarily require a teacher. In particular, learning what his body can do very often involves just the patient repetition of physical activities until the child has mastered the complete skill.

Primitive people never do formal teaching of this sort and yet their children learn to walk, to sit, to smile, to speak, and many, many more complex physical skills than do the children who grow up in our civilized society. For instance, they might learn to throw a boomerang, or to run forty miles. As responsible parents, we want to leave no stone unturned in our efforts to give our children the best start, but there's no point in becoming anxious about it, because they'll all learn what they have to know one day, sooner or later.

100

12

Acquiring Physical Skills

From birth until he is five months old, the first responses a baby makes are all essential for survival—he will cry, for example, because he is hungry. His cry is a noise sent out into space in the hope that with it food will appear. He soon learns that if he shouts loud enough, it usually does.

A baby will cry also when he is in pain. He can't deal with the discomfort, which may be a threat to his survival; he can't tell whether it is or not. If he makes enough noise, somebody ultimately comes and does something. In time he learns to recognize Mother, Father, and Grandmother (if Grandmother lives with you), as friends who can be trusted to respond to his cries and attend to his needs.

Later he will smile, not for survival but because he has learned to use his facial muscles that way. He has watched you do it, and he has watched all the people around him do it. People hardly ever approach an infant without smiling— it's a natural response to the young of the species. Soon Baby will be able to use a smile socially, as we do: to express conscious or unconscious pleasure in something or upon seeing somebody.

At about this time, too, he will discover how to hold an object. The next stage is when he uses not only his hand muscles but his arm muscles to reach for the object and pull it to him. But to start with—the first 180 times, let us say—he does it not so much because he desperately wants the object as to practice his new skill. Perfecting it involves constant repetition.

Unfortunately, in growing up, human beings lose their satisfaction in repeating the same thing over and over, which is why studying becomes progressively harder as one moves from childhood into adolescence and then adulthood. Up to the age of ten, a child loves repetition—all his games, you will notice, are concerned with it.

Consider hopscotch, or the earliest ball games he plays. You roll the ball and he rolls it back; you roll it and he rolls it back. You get bored long before he does. He'd go on for hours, until he was physically too exhausted to continue.

It's just as well, too. Unless, as a baby, he is willing to go on stretching, grasping, and pulling back until he is superb at it, he'll never get to the stage where he can pick up a pencil without consciously thinking: "See pencil; lift arm; stretch; open hand; clutch; draw back."

Crawling

Between six and ten months, one of the biggest strides often made—along with sitting up and feeding oneself, after a fashion—is crawling. It's a marvelous skill for the baby to master, because it gives him independent mobility. He can explore, he can touch things previously out of reach. It is, of course, fascinating for Mother when she's in the room watching and a nightmare when she's out of it, because her child no longer stays on the rug where she put him but takes off on some journey of his own.

How does a baby learn to crawl? Certainly not by imitation; nor by our showing him how. It requires a tremendous coordination of muscles for him to get up on his palms and knees and move. If he isn't ready yet, he will probably simply collapse.

No, I suspect that crawling is one of those instances that proves necessity can be the mother of invention. There'll come a day when he is physically strong enough and his desire to grab something beyond his radius is overwhelming. When those two prerequisites come together, he'll crawl.

Of course, many children never crawl. They go straight to walking. But if your child does show a tendency to crawl first, encourage it. It's very good for his back.

Toward the end of this age bracket and increasingly in the next, be sure you do not hinder your child's physical development (and to some extent his mental development, too) by keeping him in his carriage too much. I know that from your point of view it's a convenient, safe place for him to be. On the other hand, he cannot possibly learn to roll and crawl and stand while he's harnessed in a sitting position. So, if he's fretting or staring vacantly into space, take him out of his carriage and put him on the floor, where he can reach out for his world himself.

Standing

Too many parents think that because their child is nearly a year old, it's time he stood. So they stand him on his feet, supporting him under the arms, and then gradually let go. This is bad for a child's physical development, and it seriously frustrates the child who isn't ready to stand. It certainly doesn't teach him anything.

What you should do is to make sure the rails of his playpen are good and strong, or that you have convenient furniture about which he can use as props. When he wants to, he'll pull himself up and then stand wobbling, clutching on to the piece of furniture or whatever for safety. Encourage him, but let him be.

Long before this stage, you or a doting relative may have bought him one of the indoor swings or walkers with springs that permit Baby to bounce. I know bigger babies do love them, and I expect they do help to strengthen their legs. But, please, please, don't leave your child in his swing or walker for hours on end until he wilts with exhaustion.

I've seen this more than once. "He's as good as gold in

there," I was told by one mother. "And it means I'm free to get on with my chores . . ." I turned round to see her baby hanging asleep in his swing like a rag doll. Fifteen, twenty minutes at the most are all that I would recommend.

I find it surprising, too, that people will take a fourteen- or fifteen-month-old by the hand—Mother on one side and Father on the other—and walk him slowly along the pavement. I can't imagine what they are hoping to achieve. They aren't helping the child to walk. I'm not suggesting that the child may dislike this activity. But I suspect that he will be far too busy moving his feet to keep up with his body to examine what he feels about this activity.

A child who is ready to walk will finally dare to let go of that piece of furniture he holds when he stands, and he will grasp something else in the immediate vicinity. He may or may not get to it without mishap. He may fall down; he may cry. The contribution you as a parent should make if he does fall is to pick him up, dust him off, and take him back to the piece of furniture where he started—without very much fuss, without attaching a great deal of importance to what has happened.

Do not lift him up to comfort him and thereby remove him from the opportunity of having another try at covering that distance. Having failed once, he will find it tremendously rewarding to succeed when he tries again.

Now, once he can move from one piece of furniture to another, the next time you see him taking off, kneel down a short distance away, hold out your arms and see if he will come to Mother—not to be led to Mother by Daddy, not

105

brought to Grandma by Mother. See whether he will walk to the person whose arms he's trying to reach.

When he wants to toddle outside, by all means hold his hand—but for reassurance, not support. If he still needs your support, then it's back to the furniture with him.

There is also not much point in having your child on reins before he can walk independently, because he will then depend on them for support. Walking reins have their place—for instance, along the long corridors of a train, where he will walk much more happily than if he is led by the hand.

When, later, your child insists on walking home from the shops (better this way round, because you can carry the groceries in the stroller), it's a good idea to let him push the stroller by having him walk between its shafts. This prevents the otherwise inevitable straying of one pace forward and two to the side. And walking is less tiring for him with something to hold on to.

A word about changing from carriage to stroller. If your child likes to sit up or perhaps toddle on such expeditions, you might as well take the lighter means of transport. When you're out all day, however—perhaps for a picnic or at the zoo—in a stroller your child will have to sit up the whole time; he will probably be worn out hours before the excursion is over. How to spoil everybody's day, in one easy lesson. (Of course, if you buy a convertible stroller in which he can lie down as well, the problem's solved. But these are usually more expensive and not so easily folded away.)

Generally speaking, I wouldn't advise putting the carriage in the cellar until your child is at least fourteen months old. Until then it is safer, more comfortable, and warmer for your child. Yes—remember when you do make the transition to stroller to wrap him snugly if it's cold and tuck the blanket round his legs; he won't be nearly so protected as he was in the carriage.

Suppose He's a Lefty . . .

Finally, in this age group you may observe that your child rolls a ball to you with his left hand even when it landed nearer his right side; he picks up pebbles with his left hand—that sort of thing. Now we all know it is far more convenient to be right-handed—in our society tools are designed for right-handed people. And because of this, previous generations decided—with disastrous results—that all children should grow up to use their right hands.

Naturally, all this led to needless retardation of a child's physical development. Later still, some children who were compelled to write with their right hands suffered a block which made them unable to read. The medical term for this disability is dyslexia.

Now, having terrified you out of forcing your left-handed child to be right-handed, I can safely add that you may encourage him to be ambidextrous, to use both hands. Sometimes, not always, ask him to throw that ball with his

107

right hand, but when he says "Can't" in disgust, let him transfer it to his left.

Your pediatrician will be able to discuss your child's problem in detail with you. He may suggest other ways of helping him to be ambidextrous; he may, on the other hand, say you've a true left-hander—let him be.

I agree. I'm left-handed.

13

From Teething to Talking

Children vary widely in their reactions to the undoubtedly uncomfortable process of teething. Between six months and two years, some children seem to go through this without any noticeable discomfort; others have short periods of acute pain while a particular tooth is being cut; and some scream night after night for weeks on end while their poor parents walk up and down the floor with them.

For those of you whose children haven't reached the teething stage, let me say encouragingly that the number of children in this final group is comparatively small. It is not inevitable that you will spend weeks without a proper night's sleep. But it is only fair to add that a contented baby who's had correct feeding, no serious illness, and a stable home—and therefore emotional security—tends to react better to the discomfort of teething than does a child whose first few months have been physically and emotionally less happy.

Teething Aids

Even if you do have a difficult teether, you can do more constructive things for him than walk the floor. There are various pleasantly flavored solutions on the market that can be rubbed on the sore gums to anesthetize them mildly.

I've heard certain authorities say crushingly that these solutions and jellies are of no medicinal value. I can't say; I'm not a pediatrician or a druggist. But I do know that babies like the taste of them; they also recognize that Mother is doing something to bring comfort rather than just frantically sobbing along with them. This is behavior guaranteed to persuade any sufferer that he's beyond hope.

You've seen teething rings for the baby to chew on—rather as the teething puppy uses a chair leg. These rings are generally made of plastic, which from time to time can be sterilized; but in fact any hard, smooth material would serve just as well. My mother-in-law gave her children her solid gold bracelet to bite on—it still bears the tooth marks.

How about a piece of zwieback to chew on? Well, I have clear memories of what must have been a ton of half-chewed bits of zwieback that I swept up from the carpet and dug out of the corners of armchairs, so I have serious doubts about their value. However, if you find your child likes something of the sort, then I'd advise a piece of bread baked to crispness in the oven, or thoroughly toasted. This won't fill him up to the same extent as zwieback and won't be another sweet thing in his diet.

If all this treatment isn't sufficient, consult your doctor. He may think it necessary to prescribe a sedative, especially if your baby's discomfort is robbing you and your husband of sleep. Oh dear—in case I've confused you, the sedative is for the baby. Certainly you cannot leave him lying there screaming with pain while you try to sleep. For one thing, no mother could relax under such circumstances, and for another, the poor child would feel abandoned in his misery.

There can be side effects to teething: your baby's digestion may be upset, he may develop diaper rash, he may even have bouts of vomiting, earache, or nasal infection—especially when the back teeth emerge. Be on the lookout for these upsets, but I sincerely hope that your child—and consequently you—will be among the lucky ones to whom growing a tooth is no worse than growing fingernails.

The First Word

Talking is originally a physical skill—that of reproducing a sound. Only later does it become the mental skill of communication. There are children who reach both stages

111

simultaneously. Having been silent to the age of three, they suddenly speak in whole sentences. But this is rare, and most children utter little sounds from the time they are a few weeks old.

Over the months to come, these sounds will become speech patterns—*la-da-da-na* sort of thing—until finally the child will come out with a word, generally a familiar one that is easy to pronounce. In the case of my own eldest, it was, not surprisingly, "Mommy."

When Tina was nine months old, we were spending our vacation with some country friends who had a dog. It was a lovely summer, and I used to feed Tina in her high chair out in the garden. Anything she didn't finish, the dog was always ready and willing to finish for her.

In fact, it got to the point where I automatically put a bowl next to Tina's chair, and the dog would sit there wagging her tail waiting for the goodies to drop. The dog's name was Dusty, and my cry of "Dusty! Dusty! Come, Dusty!" became a ritual before each of Tina's meals. Then one day she beat me to it. "Dutty! Dutty! Dutty!" she called as I brought out her food.

It's a thrilling moment for every mother. It's also cute that children will say "Dutty" instead of "Dusty," or "foobah" instead of sugar. It's tempting for you to start saying "foobah" yourself. One little indulgence is all right. But keep it at that. The object is for your child to learn your language, not the other way round.

Although I can sincerely claim that I have never compared my children's physical development with other children's, I did fall into the trap of comparing them with each other. So I was secretly concerned when Merle didn't speak at nine months, at a year, at practically two years.

We talked to her regularly in proper language, which is all any parent can do to teach her child to speak. (Mirrors, candles, fingers against lips—these are for the dumb or retarded child and should be introduced by experts.) Merle, in turn, communicated with all sorts of sounds of her own. Since we understood what these noises indicated, there wasn't any practical problem.

Then, when she reached two, my husband and I had to go away for six weeks and leave her in the care of a governess. On our return, we rang the front-door bell and heard the patter of Merle's feet in the hall. She opened the door and said, quite clearly, "Hello, Mommy and Daddy." And she's hardly stopped talking since. Merle, the late talker, is the most articulate of my three children.

You see, she'd needed the impetus of someone who didn't understand her various noises to force her to say proper words. But a long separation is too drastic a method of getting a child to talk. I'd prefer to wait, patiently. After all, some people find pronunciation more difficult than do others. For instance, take the French *oui* sound. Some students say it right the first time they hear it, others still get it wrong after years of listening to Maurice Chevalier and Sacha Distel.

14

Helping Your Child to Talk

How do you teach your child to talk? To answer this question, we have to return to what I said earlier about constantly reminding ourselves that we are dealing not with a creature of a different species, but with a human being in miniature. Cooing and gooing at a baby may entertain him momentarily, but it's condescending and certainly doesn't stimulate him. Talking to him in ordinary language, not baby talk, will help him to talk clearly later on—and just as important, condition us to think of him as someone we can talk to.

To a new baby you should at first talk about the immediate activities in which he and you are involved.

About eating, for instance, you can say: "Come on. This is breakfast. How about having your breakfast?" After that: "Now we've got you changed, don't you think it's time you had a nap? Would you like to play—or would you really like to go to your crib straight away?"

I'm all in favor of using "we" in talking to an infant, of saying, "*We* will do this" and "Let's play." Obviously this won't work in every situation. It's definitely "you" and not "we" who will be going into that crib for a nap. But aim for a friendly, equal relationship.

Avoid Deliberate Repetition

There is very little value in pointing to an object and saying its name over and over again in the hope that your child will suddenly repeat the word after you. Children learn what things are called, and how to pronounce the names, because they're familiar. If you always say when you go to a particular closet, "Let's see what we can find in the closet; let's get out your blue coat," he will ultimately say "closet" and "coat."

In the same way he will learn to name the parts of his body because you are talking about washing his face and drying his hands and buttoning his sweater to keep his chest warm, and so on. You don't have to intone, again and again, "Eyes. Eyes. Eyes. Eyes . . ."

115

Learning a Foreign Language

And then, there is the question of a foreign language. I am sure most parents—particularly parents of older children who are taking languages at school—must be aware of the difficulties of meeting French or German or Spanish for the first time at thirteen. Of course, it's difficult. Thirteen is the wrong age at which to begin.

The right age for a child to learn any language—a language, let us say, spoken fluently by one or both parents—is when he is learning to speak his first language. It has been demonstrated over and over that many children can learn to speak two or three languages simultaneously before the age of two. Yes, they do mix up the words and use the verbs in French and the nouns in English; but they sort out the various languages pretty quickly.

Admittedly, they won't learn the grammar; but you are not teaching your baby or toddler the grammar of his own language either. Between birth and three years of age, he first learns to say words and then he learns to form sentences in imitation of the way you speak. It's many years later before he is able to understand subject and indirect object. The same pattern is true for a foreign language. So, if you want your child to be bilingual, or multi-lingual, the time to start to speak another language to him is in earliest babyhood—by means of songs, poems, and the ordinary communication about food and diapers and Teddy bears and flowers.

I learned to speak a second language in two weeks

when I was three. I had to, because I was staying in a country where no one spoke my own language. Unfortunately, I promptly forgot my original tongue. Then, when I saw my father again, for a while I couldn't talk to him. But this rarely happens and my circumstances were rather extraordinary.

By the way, do bear in mind that you can forget a language faster than you can learn it if you do not use it constantly. Many a mother who studied French through college can now remember only *La plume de ma tante,* which is of little use in most conversations in France.

About Slanguage

What do you do when your child of between three and five comes in from play with some choice phrase picked up from a companion? I suggest you do nothing directly. If you correct him at that moment, you hammer that phrase into his mind forever. He can use it as a weapon; he's bound to use it on all occasions when you want him to speak properly.

The thing to do is to maintain your standard of speech at home, and he will automatically learn to do so too, providing you have a good relationship with him. The only reason why the average child from a "nice" home will speak badly is because he was, consciously to begin with and then unconsciously, resisting his parents during the period in which he formed his speech patterns.

117

If you are forever correcting your child when he is speaking, you will achieve the opposite result. If you merely maintain your own standard of speech at home, you will find he will soon, all by himself, make a sharp distinction. He will speak with you as you speak, and with his friends as he has to speak to survive as a member of the tribe rather than an outsider. It is unfair to expect more of him. So, there's no need to correct pronunciation; on the contrary, it is undesirable to do so.

Correcting Grammar

What is desirable is to correct grammar, and how to do this for the child under five is perhaps worth mentioning also.

If your child comes in bursting to tell you something— it may be trivial to you but all-important to him—and all his words jumble up, and the verbs and nouns go into the wrong places and he says "me" when it should be "mine," don't correct him in the middle and thus cut off his flow of speech. Let him express himself as he will, to get the story out, so that its full content is not undermined by your constant, patient, "No, dear, not that way." That's a good way to make him inarticulate in maturity.

After he has told you the story, you should, in the course of discussing it, use the right phrases. Try as little as possible to do this on a *correction* basis; do it rather on a *correct* basis. If you virtually retell the story to him properly

118

in conversation, he will learn to express himself as grammatically as you do. And in the meantime you won't have made him self-conscious and frustrated.

I wish more teachers realized this. How often they stifle imagination and enthusiasm in their anxiety to have their pupils use the right past participle or whatever. I remember that my daughter Merle—admittedly when she was much older than the children we're discussing in this book—once wrote a remarkable essay. The subject was Law and Order, and she'd chosen a fascinating incident from World War II. Her essay was vivid, it was alive, it flowed. Yet her teacher's only comment was "Punctuation!" Crushing and discouraging!

Obviously, as your child's awareness of his surroundings increases, he will be able to express this increased awareness in words, and you must be ready and willing to address him with an enriched vocabulary. Don't be afraid of using words he won't understand. Quite the reverse—do. He will learn more words quickly if you are in the habit of using a fairly extensive vocabulary.

Talking is indeed verbal communication. But it is not enough just to be able to verbalize a need like "More milk, please." What enriches life is the ability to express ideas, to share them with others.

15

Learning Coordination

The average child learns more new things in his first two years than he does in the rest of his life. By three, certainly, he has mastered the physical skills which are an end in themselves. He can walk and run, and so on. Yet, the things he learns between three and five are just as important, and in a wider sense.

For instance, it is comparatively valueless to learn to kick a ball, although it could have a practical application: one could become a professional football player and end up earning an awful lot of money. But, generally speaking, the skill itself is interesting and useful only if we consider it in the framework of handling our environment, of being able to coordinate thought, eye, and leg. In the same way, we don't encourage our children to cut up sticky paper with scissors as the first step to being a designer. We are teaching them to manipulate a tool, any tool.

Tricycles develop their leg muscles. Incidentally, a tricycle might instill road sense in a child for the car he'll have one day—but, having seen the reckless way most tots zoom about on their three-wheelers, I tremble at the very idea.

Don't be perturbed if a toy or tool manufactured for the statistically average child within a certain age range doesn't suit your child. Regardless of what it says on the box, he may be too old for it, or too young.

Don't immediately assume the worst. I realize it's disappointing to the fond aunt who gave him the gift, but he simply may not be interested in developing that particular activity at this time, whether it's fitting objects into correspondingly shaped openings, handling paints, or finding out how to fill a bucket with sand and build a castle. He may return to it later on his own, or he may need the company of other children to stimulate his desire to acquire that skill.

Swimming

While we're discussing physical skill, I should say a word about swimming. You may have read in magazines and newspapers the claims of experts that any child can learn to swim before he's two, that it is valuable to teach him to swim before he's two, even that it's essential to teach him to swim before he's two.

Well, is there a right age for teaching a child to swim? My answer to that is the same as to every similar question in this chapter—yes, when he's ready. And he can be ready anywhere from the age of two on, given the sort of environment in which swimming is easily possible. Much, of course, depends on the climate, and, unless one lives near water, on the availability of a swimming pool. But if the right conditions exist, and you are certain your child wants to swim, then by all means try teaching him.

A two-year-old who clings fearfully to your neck when *you* are in three feet of water is not ready to swim. But a two-year-old who, safely supported on your arm, is willing to splash in that same water, might be. Many children under five are terrified when they first confront the vast expanse of the sea or of a huge lake. They are genuinely frightened standing in water just over their ankles if it's at all choppy. Yet their fathers will march them in, struggling, to paddle. This is no good. The child won't think of it as fun at all; he will simply grow more petrified as the water grows deeper.

Ordeal by Water

Before a child can possibly enjoy bathing, it is essential for him to become friendly with this new element. The

122

principle that any animal will swim if you throw him in the deep end—and if he doesn't you're there to rescue him— isn't the way to teach a child the joys of swimming.

As a rule, mothers realize this. But fathers find it undesirable, even weak, when their child—especially a son—is scared of water. It's silly, of course; we're all scared of something. But with the right kind of handling—"When you've finished collecting shells, if you want to join us down there for a dip, we'd be glad to have you"—this is one fear the child can gradually outgrow. So, if you think your husband belongs to the category I describe, you might like to leave this page open where he can see it . . .

Incidentally, suppose your child is at the point where he's prepared to move his arms and legs if you support his belly. If he says, "Don't let go; promise you won't let go," don't break your word even if you're sure he'll actually swim if you do let him go. That could destroy his confidence in the water forever. *Let him take his time.* Make this a general rule, and your child will develop many skills of his own, skills that may go far beyond yours and those of his brothers and sisters. My children, for example, swim very well, while I just about manage to dog-paddle in the shallow end of the pool. They also play a good game of tennis, and I don't.

It is just possible that you have an infant prodigy with a gift for music that far surpasses anything you've ever dreamed for him. As his parents, you will be proud—and pleased that someone you love can achieve such fulfillment.

But let him take his time. He himself will lead you when he is ready. Just stand by and see that he has what he needs. The rule is equally important when your child begins to develop mentally.

16

Learning Through Play

Adults tend to think of play as something children do because they aren't old enough to go to school or to work. But our division between work and play is artificial: It's like saying "Planting is fun but weeding is work." Actually every effort a human being of any age makes can be described as work.

A baby is working, and working hard, if he's taking milk from the breast or the bottle. He is working when he's excreting and the effort is obvious. He is working when he is sitting on the floor examining the curtain hem. Both his mind and his body are involved when he is finding his toes and grasping with his hands.

Mother, Don't Smother

It is essential for a child to explore and to learn to control his immediate surroundings. This environment should become wider and more complex as he grows older—and if you don't interrupt and inhibit his work, it will. Now, this doesn't mean a child should be permitted to do whatever he pleases. It is part of the learning process to acknowledge that there are certain things one should not do and certain things one simply cannot do.

As a loving parent you will want to stop your child from hurting himself. But don't overprotect him. Supervise what he does, naturally; you cannot allow him to stick his fingers into a live socket. But, on the other hand, he must discover that there *are* sockets and why we protect him from them.

Similarly, he will never find out why a knife or scissors can hurt him unless he is allowed to use them. Obviously, you will not choose your sharpest steak knives for teaching your child to cut his bread. But show him the blade and let him know he'd cut himself if he used it improperly. The same with scissors; let him have his own paper scissors and keep your dressmaking shears out of reach.

If we are sensible, we allow our children to use ordinary household implements as part of their play activity, so that they will learn how to handle them. Using dustpan and brush to tidy the floor, for instance, is desirable. Hitting brother or sister on the head with either dustpan or brush is not. But no child will ever appreciate what a dustpan and a brush are for if he's never permitted to touch them.

126

This also applies to climbing stairs, or learning how a window opens. He must be taught. We mustn't simply put him into an environment regardless of its hazards and let him take his chances—he could fall down those stairs or out that window. Yet keeping him in as safe an environment as we can devise—a playpen, for example—is almost as dangerous. One day he's got to come out. (Not that I'm against playpens for half-hour stretches. They're ideal while you load the washing machine or change the beds. But never limit your child's horizons by keeping him confined in one constantly.)

When we consider how we can best help our children to develop mentally, we must always remember: never force, never make him compete with some other child, never attempt to make a child do things because we used to do them at that age. Instead, go along with the child's own efforts to do what he seems ready to do.

Learning by Observation

There are so many things that your baby absorbs almost without your being aware of it. He is learning when simply watching the family: you doing the household chores, Father working with tools, the older children at play—all this is part of Baby's learning process.

He needs the companionship, too. He doesn't need only to have his physical wants taken care of; companionship is part of what he requires for survival—not just for immediate survival but for the future. Gradually, of course, he'll seek companionship not just from you and your husband but from a number of people. This is the great advantage of growing up in a family, because he'll get companionship automatically at different times and in different ways from lots of people. He needs to be played with, and he needs to have things that will stimulate his interest.

17

The Psychology of Play

The child's play helps him to understand the world around
him and to form his own ideas about it. There are many
theories about why children play, and especially why they
play certain games. Working out the underlying motivation
at its deepest level lies in the territory of child psychology,
not in the realm of parenthood. I think it is sufficient to say
here that fundamentally children play because it is natural
for a normal, healthy being to engage in activities that use
his brain and his body, rather than lying around like a
vegetable all day.

Unless there is a real emotional disturbance—in which
case play becomes something entirely different—or unless

the child is urged to do things in the name of play that he doesn't like doing, he will enjoy it. It should go without saying that you don't force a son who is not athletic onto the baseball field, or force a restless daughter to sit and sew. As we said earlier: have the stimuli available, but don't press them on your child.

As a matter of fact, it's hard to persuade a small child to do something that doesn't appeal to him. I know a number of children under five who love music and who play beautifully in nursery school bands. But however many guitars, drums, triangles, recorders and the like may be available at home or school, the child who is not interested in music will not avail himself of them, at least at that time. But, like toys, the instruments may be rejected now and enthusiastically adopted later.

When He's Ready

My son got a building construction set, a simple one, as a present when he was four. He could not have been less interested. Oh yes, he threw the bits around—and lost most of them—but made no attempt to construct anything that resembled the pictures on the superb colored sheet of instructions. I tried to work on it with him. No. He did all sorts of other things with the pieces—arranged them according to colors, or shuffled them, but nothing the kit was intended for. When he was about eight, he saw the identical kit in a friend's house in the hands of a younger child. He was fascinated by it and accused me of never having provided him with one. He refused to believe he'd had the very same thing four years earlier.

So don't assume that because your child shows no desire to build things when he's four, he will never be interested in building. From time to time, see that the material to make something is available for him to turn to when he is ready. The same with musical instruments.

Toys Are For Children

Another thing: your child's toys are not your property. They're his, and if he doesn't want to play with them, that's his business. If he doesn't want to use his toys the way the manufacturers or you think they should be used, it is his right not to. This does not mean you should permit your child to damage and break toys at will just because he owns them. Destructiveness for its own sake is irresponsible and self-indulgent.

This applies also to playthings that are not strictly toys—pencils, crayons, paints, paper, blackboards, for example. If he wants to play trains with them instead of using them for drawing, it's his privilege. But he should not be allowed to discard them in the middle of the floor to be stepped on and broken.

131

18

Toys for Baby

In talking to parents while writing this book, I have come to the reluctant conclusion that play materials and toys constitute a real problem. It's not merely a matter of money but of knowing what to buy and where to find it, and what sorts of things are suitable at what stage.

Many store-bought toys are of little, if any, interest to a small child. Many toys break disappointingly when a sturdy toddler drops them, or they are for *looking at*, not for *doing things with*, which is the prime requisite of any play material, toy or game. Toys are not means by which we keep our children quiet. They are tools for learning about the world, and for expressing the ideas such learning stimulates. The books that you read to young children also come under this heading.

Toys Need Not Be Expensive

I can only suggest generally what will be most suitable at the various age levels. You as parents must choose what to buy, make, or borrow (large toys, for example, such as a swing or see-saw). A lot will depend on how handy Mother and Father are with tools, paint brush, and needle.

Don't hesitate to beg for empty cartons, boxes, and the like from shops—they are often only too glad to give away what would otherwise clutter up their storage space or raise their refuse collection bills. Neighbors and friends, too, are also often happy to get rid of what they consider rubbish, things your child might enjoy investigating. A lot of money is not a necessity when you're trying to supply your child with toys that are fun to explore.

Sensory Awareness

A child up to six months old is interested in the sensations that he feels as a result of playing with things. The development of your child's sensory awareness of the different substances that he encounters is important and enjoyable to him.

133

Consider the pictures on the wall in the room where he sleeps. Pleasant pictures of animals, real or imaginary, are an excellent idea, for they give him something interesting to look at rather than just a plain painted wall. (Colorful nursery wallpapers are a good alternative.)

Mobiles can be bought or simply made by stringing together some brightly colored and perhaps shiny materials and household objects light enough to move in any breeze. You can, for example, string lightly crushed colored tissue paper, cut-up drinking straws, and small balls of foil on a piece of thin cord; suspend the mobile in front of the window.

Rattles can be made by using strong nylon cord to string together eight to twelve old-fashioned key rings (1″ in diameter). A different rattle—it's a different shape and makes a different sound—can be made by stringing together all the old keys you never use. (Note: wash them well before using them and wash again at intervals.)

At first, suspend the rattles horizontally a good distance from your baby's crib, and jiggle them now and then to make them jingle. At four months and upwards he will want to play with the rattles himself, and they will be chewed, thrown on the floor, and generally fully investigated.

The fluffy duck that so many parents suspend from the hood of the carriage and the all-too-familiar strings of beads that go across the hood not only are dull but also are too close to his eyes.

Safe objects for baby to hold include napkin rings, empty adhesive-tape rolls, empty light-bulb cartons, Mother's silver bracelet, teaspoons, and the cardboard cylinders from toilet rolls. Put any one of them in his hand and leave him to experience it; it will fall out of his hand after a few seconds. His span of attention is short, so repeat the operation; give him the object several times. After a few days, change the rules of the game. Place the same object just within his reach, and if he is ready to play the more advanced version (from about three-and-a-half months onward), he will pick the object up himself. It still will fall from his hand after a few seconds. So repeat, repeat, repeat.

Specific Recommendations

Baby will enjoy bouncing on Mother's knee to rhythmic music, or dancing to its beat in Mother's arms.

He will enjoy flexible toys, such as friendly-looking stuffed animals (young children get frightened of fierce-looking wolves). The flexibility of such toys is useful in developing a young child's manipulative skills. But watch out that he doesn't try to bend the kitten's legs.

Stuffed animals, bought or homemade, should be small, no more than 12" to 15" tall. Your baby will probably not play with them, but will surely welcome their company in his crib or carriage.

Collect small tins such as tobacco tins (if your husband smokes a pipe and favors the English tobaccos that come in tins) and fill them with sand, or gravel, or dried peas, or old buttons, or beads. Seal the tins well by covering the edges

135

with scotch tape or masking tape, and paint them with non-toxic paints in different colors. These will prove "educational" because not only will your child learn to distinguish the various sounds they make, but he will also learn gradually to pile the tins up.

As for drums, don't buy the tin kind. Their sound is poor and will hinder him from developing a musical ear. It will be better simply to give him your aluminum saucepan and a wooden spoon (not that an aluminum saucepan is particularly tuneful). Actually, the best drum of all is an open-ended cylinder (made from a can that has had its ends removed with a clean-cutting safety can opener), over which rubber sheeting has been stretched.

As for bells, Indian brass bells are my favorites and can often be found in nursery and gift shops. Half a dozen brass bells attached to a circle of tape are even more fun because each bell sounds a different note.

Baby's rattle of old key-rings makes a great toy for playing tug-of-war, an enjoyable game that will help him to develop muscles.

Three or four identical corn-flakes cartons (big or little) make ideal blocks for a young child.

Empty plastic containers and Jello molds of different sizes that fit one within another will teach him about the inter-relationship of objects.

Bean bags are splendid for learning about textures and sounds, and for throwing. You can make bean bags out of lots of different colored and textured materials. (Look through your scrap bag for velvet, silk, leatherette, corduroy, etc.) Fill small thick plastic bags with peas or buttons or pebbles, leaving enough space at the top for them to remain mobile and make sounds. Then place the plastic bags inside the cloth bags and sew up firmly.

19

Games for Baby

Toys are not the only things that amuse a baby and enrich his experience. He likes kicking diaperless on the floor. His own fingers and toes make fascinating playmates. Being gently splashed and later splashing himself in the bath is pleasurable. He enjoys the movements of a rocking chair, his carriage, or the family car. He loves to watch the play of light and the movement of leaves.

The Age-Old Games

At this point, all those games that mothers have played with their children from time immemorial are especially important to his growth: bouncing Baby on a knee, singing nursery rhymes to him; reaching-and-withdrawing games.

Babies learn to play reaching-and-withdrawing games very easily from about four to five months. You hold out, let us say, a finger and wait for Baby to grasp it. You then withdraw the finger and wait for Baby's hand to come forward to reach for your finger again. And when he does reach out for your finger, you take it away again. A similar version of this is pulling a rattle up, and then Baby pulling it down. You pull it up; he pulls it down.

I know these games of repetition are not madly exciting for you, but your baby loves them. They also teach him what response you are expecting, and that is something we all have to learn. In all sorts of everyday situations we have to know what response someone is expecting from us; so the sooner your baby can start to anticipate this, the better.

The Need to Communicate

Between six months and one year, your child will begin to reach out deliberately to extend his discovery instead of merely accepting the little world that closely surrounds him. He will also begin to communicate—not only about a need but also because he actively wishes to form a relationship.

He will begin to throw things out of his carriage and, as soon as you've picked them up and given them back to him, hurl them out again. He hasn't dropped the Teddy bear or whatever. He has thrown it on the ground deliberately in the hope that somebody, and he hopes it will be you, will pick up the Teddy and stay there and pick it up again and again and again. I know it's arduous and a bore for an adult. I've done it for many weary hours for many children, including my own.

After five minutes or so, you will probably have to say, "Well, that's that. This is the last time. I can't go on playing with you any more. I have to cook the dinner." But for a while do accept this sort of activity as an attempt at communication on the part of your baby.

With increasing mobility and an increasing desire to communicate, a child between one and two will still enjoy the toys he had before, but the gradual introduction of some new ones and new activities will help him to develop further.

One of his favorite activities will be the game of give and take. All through the day he will like giving you an object and having you give it back to him, again and again. It may be a rattle, or a woolly bear, or something small such as a scrap of paper he's found on the floor. This is *nonverbal communication.*

When you send a friend a present for her birthday, you are not, I hope, doing so only because you don't want to offend her, or because she'll let you know later that you forgot. You do it because you wish to communicate your good wishes by means of a gift. Similarly, when you offer someone a chocolate, a cup of coffee, or a drink, you are communicating on a nonverbal level. The child who is not old enough to communicate verbally uses these games of give and take to communicate.

And if your child hands you a tack or some other dangerous object he's found, don't snatch it away hysterically. Quietly accept it and replace it with something safer in order not to interrupt the communication.

Here are some other activities for Baby:

PUTTING IN AND TAKING OUT In front of your child, fill a shoe box with a number of safe objects—teaspoons, screw-top lids, small plastic jars, perhaps an old but clean purse (empty!). Put the lid on the box. The child will enjoy taking the lid off and emptying the box. Repeat over and over again. You will get bored long before he does. Later, he will enjoy sample pieces of linoleum, Formica, or even small decorative tiles to "mail" through a slit in the lid of the box. (Make sure the slit is big enough.) Around about the age of two years, he will be able to "mail" different shapes in different openings.

PAINTING Yes, it *is* messy, but from about eighteen months onward it's very valuable. Instead of paint, though, use a small blob of chocolate pudding, syrup, or orange juice (one color only at first) and just put it on the tray of his high-chair. Don't show him what to do, and *don't combine this with his meal*. He will soon find out. The different textures provide a useful sensory education and prepare him for play with paints later.

THE MAZE A crawler will love exploring a simple maze built from large empty cardboard cartons without lids or bottoms. (You need space for this!) He will have even more

141

fun if someone crawls in front of or behind him—great entertainment, incidentally, for youthful uncles and aunts. (He will also enjoy playing with empty egg cartons, plastic shampoo bottles, yogurt containers, and large cardboard boxes from the supermarkets.)

MOBILE TOYS   When loving relatives ask you to suggest presents, remind them to make sure that the Teddy bears and other toys they bring are not too big for the child. This applies also to mechanical toys such as tricycles. Always keep in mind the size of the child relative to the toy, particularly if he is still unsteady on his feet.

WATER PLAY   When he is in the bath, offer him a strainer, preferably plastic, and an empty plastic shampoo bottle. The former, of course, won't hold water, while the latter will. Not only are these "toys" fun, but they will teach him something about the different ways in which liquids can be poured.

BALLS   Look for the foam rubber ones with soft indents; they're easier for him to grasp to throw. He hasn't the skill yet to catch.

SMALL SHOPPING BASKET   This will be useful for carting things about. He will find his own objects to put in it.

HAMMER AND PEGS   These will teach the child to create a mechanical effect with a tool.

142

HOMEMADE JIGSAW PUZZLE Take a large rectangle (18″ × 2′) of thick cardboard or plywood and from it cut a 3″ diameter circle, a square, a rectangle, a regular triangle (all of similar size to the circle). Paint them in bright but different colors with non-toxic paint. Then paint the whole board another color and leave it up to your child to find out what fits in where.

CHRISTMAS AND BIRTHDAY CARDS Save them. Most children enjoy playing with them because they are so attractive.

PICTURE BOOKS Give him stiff-board books with vivid illustrations of real animals, cars, trees, trains, people—not the new books that look as if an under-five-year-old had painted them. The story is of no importance, because you won't be reading it to him at this age, anyway. Many children can handle a book with paper pages; if your child has one, teach him not to tear it. Old newspaper is for that purpose. But books with cloth pages are a good idea.

THREADING GAME Give him brightly colored rings to thread on a rod, or empty toilet roll cylinders on a piece of rope.

GLOVE PUPPET I had one while I was working in the children's ward of a hospital. My puppet gave out medicines, tucked small people in for the night, and generally dispensed comfort. By the time I had children of my own, that particular puppet had passed on, but a friend got me a glove-puppet monkey to replace him. His body was fur and

143

his face and hands were made of a soft plastic material. Monkey became my most valuable ally. It was he who was obeyed when the current young one decided to oppose Mother. He told rhymes, sang songs, fell into the bath, and could sit on a chest of drawers in the children's room to watch over them and keep them safe from bad dreams.

His particular value lay in the fact that I made him do things, not *they*. I owned him, but he was a friend to my children. He ended his days in a nursery school where my son had been a happy pupil for two years; but I recently bought a new one, because my grand-daughter, who is in this age group, was coming to visit.

The Need for a Companion

After about fourteen months, your child will increasingly need someone to play with him. Try not to be inhibited about singing to him, telling him rhymes, simple stories, and playing as he plays. Your housework should be done when and as you can, but it should not take precedence over the need your child has for your attention.

Between two and three, most children enjoy playing near other children, but not with them. Playing together will not take place yet unless the other child or children are much older, and replace the adult playmate he is accustomed to. This is also the time when mothers will complain that "he is constantly under my feet." Of course, he is. He now needs less sleep during the day and he loves doing things when you do them—often with your broom and your pots. At this stage, miniature household implements will not do, only yours. The miniature ones are used much later for conscious make-believe. He will still enjoy many of the toys he had before, but now he will be able to use them more skillfully.

Toys and games should have a definite home—a box, a cabinet, a place where they can be stored conveniently and where your child can put them away himself. If you have chosen as your cabinet one that can be reached only by an adult, you've chosen badly. It must be a place easily accessible to your child, because from two (if not earlier) onward, he will want to choose his own playthings rather than settle for the ones you put out for him. And as soon as he is physically capable of reaching into this cabinet or box to get his toys out, he's also capable of helping you to put them away again.

The overindulgent mother feels that play is what her child should do and work is what she should do. Therefore, she feels, the work of putting the toys away is something she should undertake (it will only take a few minutes, she argues). This mother is not training her child correctly, because she is failing to teach him self-discipline and to look after his possessions.

20

Games and Toys for

When He's Older

When your child is between two and three years of age, he is ready for additional games and toys that will develop him.

SAND-AND-WATER-PLAY   Sandboxes, indoors and outdoors, and a basin or pail in which to sail boats and float ducks are musts—not on the living room carpet, of course, but in the kitchen, bathroom, or playroom—any place that can be easily swept or mopped. For water play, the water should be about the temperature of Baby's bath. Besides boats and ducks, provide a collection of funnels, plastic glasses, "squirty" bottles, spoons, and corks, and then let him find whatever else he wants to put into the water, as long as it isn't glass or sharp metal. A basin or pail is ever so much safer than letting him play in the bathtub.

A similar container can be used as a miniature sandbox. Beach sand is good if you live near the seashore; otherwise, buy well-washed builder's sand. Supply bucket, spade, empty coffee tins, spoons and scoops, small gardening tools, strainers and sifters, cookie cutters, toy cars, and trucks. If the sandbox is left out-of-doors, protect it against cats and dogs with a fine wire mesh.

MODELING   A good cheap substitute for modeling clay can be made of:

$\frac{1}{2}$ pound flour
$\frac{1}{4}$ cup of salt
1 tablespoon cooking oil
powder paint (from an art supply shop)
hot water, to mix to suitable consistency

Use one color to begin with, and then provide a second color when your child seems to need it.

PAINTING   Provide some place other than your walls for your child to paint to his heart's content. For his first finger-painting efforts, thicken powder paint with flour to make it go further, and give him some old newspapers for a canvas.

Later, large sheets of ordinary kitchen paper, the kind you use to line drawers and shelves, make ideal painting paper. Kitchen paper provides the right surface, and it is cheap. Pin or nail the paper to a board at least $3' \times 2'$ in size. Children find scraps of notepaper inhibiting and prefer

147

big fields for their scrawls. (If your child proves to be an exception to this rule and prefers to create miniatures, well then, this is something to recognize and act upon; but as a general rule, the bigger the better.)

Not the finest brushes, please, because his manual dexterity to handle small things develops much later. So start with finger painting, and when he is almost three introduce him to painting with large brushes.

PEDAL TOYS   Pedaling (both the circular motion on a tricycle and the fore-and-after motion in a pedal car) is a new skill and helps him to learn to control a means of transport. A rocking horse on casters is an exciting toy and much more interesting than a conventional static one.

MODEL CARS   Cars, buses, etc., large and small, should be chosen for sturdiness, not for their value as scale models. And buy friction toys, not clockwork ones.

MEDIUM-SIZED BALL   He will need this for kicking and throwing, and beginning to learn to catch.

DOLLS   Rag dolls only at this stage. They are the continuation of the small stuffed companion in the crib, and are valuable for the two- to three-year-old because they represent a human companion. Don't expect a child at this age to play house.

MUSIC   This is also the age at which your child will begin to express music instead of just listening to it. A tambourine (of wood and parchment rather than the toy-shop variety) is not expensive and children enjoy the combined drum/bell effect they create with it. If you are a pianist, try some simple nursery rhymes on the piano and leave the tambourine someplace where your child can readily pick it up. If you do not play the piano, try instead some suitable music programs on the radio or play records, and see what encourages the best response in your child.

Maracas are good rhythm instruments, as are bells, two toy bricks banged together, and gongs.

As your child reaches three years or older, he will enjoy singing and will be able to pronounce the words clearly as he sings. He will particularly like to sing together with other children or with you. (Those all-too-frequent solo performances for guests in your home, however, will only make him self-conscious, and will often embarrass the visitor.)

I have a treasured memory to this day. Whenever I hear the song, "Dites-moi Pourquoi," I don't remember the charming children of *South Pacific* singing it. I hear instead my three-year-old and six-year-old singing to the record while beating a tambourine and ringing a bracelet with small bells sewn onto it.

21

Appreciation Is Crucial

Always display your child's artistic efforts. There is nothing so discouraging to a child as the mother in whose "nice" house there is no room for such junk. On the other hand, don't bore your visitors by expounding on the artistic merit of your child's efforts. Loving grandparents will need no persuasion to admire the art, and you don't need confirmation that your child is another Vermeer—at least at this stage.

Bestow approval but not effusive praise for what is obviously a clumsy first attempt. Of course, you don't say it's poor. But it's almost as disheartening for a child to receive extravagant praise—this is often interpreted as an unconscious effort to show how superior the adult is. Children have their own standards, and they can judge if something is really as good as Mother says, or if, on the other hand, it should have gained a little more approval— not admiration—than it did.

Show His Work

Everyone who has created something likes to see it displayed; so choose a wall, preferably in the kitchen, where he can go and look at it and where he knows you can see it, too. The painting or drawing will undoubtedly be followed by another, and when the replacement arrives, you can take down the original.

You don't have to fill all the walls of your house with what is to an adult very often meaningless scribbling. But pin up each one just for a while. Have it there for him and for you—not for the neighbors.

Throughout his life, not only for his first five years, your child will create things to give you. However odd they may be, they should be treated as something you value—not more precious than your diamond ring, but precious nevertheless because they are gifts from him.

A child can be very perceptive. He quickly realizes that the small box he made is standing on the mantelpiece because you don't quite know what to do with it, yet haven't the heart to throw it away. Your child will want to see it in use. Well, try to make use of it—perhaps as a pin box or a paperweight. Don't put it away in a drawer, perhaps to be sentimental over in twenty years time, when it won't matter any more. *Appreciate it now.*

Setting an Example

Moreover, you're setting your child an example. He should learn early that a present *he* has been given that he's not very keen on should nevertheless be treated with some respect for the giver. It's not only a matter of "please" and "thank you" and writing letters of gratitude. That will come later. But even while he is very young, he is capable of making some attempt to let the giver know the present is being used and enjoyed.

I've heard many husbands say, "My wife's got drawers full of things that I've given her that she's never used. It makes me hate to choose another present . . ." How sad. The reason for such rejection often is rooted in infancy. If a person's gifts to his or her parents have been treated this way—and it doesn't mean the parents were negligent, only that they didn't understand—then it's small wonder this person never learned the joy of giving and receiving.

The way you react now in regard to your child is important for the whole of his life, and for his relationships with people long after you have any direct responsibility for him. Again, we come back to the importance of treating him as you would wish him to treat others later.

152

22

Developing His Potential

Between the ages of three and five, it will be convenient, I hope, for your child to attend a nursery school or day care center. If not, you can take your cue from the wealth of play materials offered in those places.

In either case, watch the directions in which your child's interests develop and supply the equipment that will help him to extend his world. Beware of giving in to whims, the toy garage or the battery-operated miniature washing-machine. In general, it is better to give him small things at intervals throughout the year that you are pretty sure will stimulate him than to save up for that one big present for Christmas or his birthday.

Support, Don't Direct

I cannot emphasize strongly enough how wrong I think it is to attempt to steer children along lines not suitable for them. If you are determined, let us say, to make your child into another Mozart, but unfortunately the child is tone deaf and only interested in motor cars, then you are in serious trouble.

Rather than make your child fit a preconceived pattern, observe him so that you are constantly ready to assist him, or to seek the expert assistance you are unable to give him. In this way, you will develop his potential in the direction he has chosen. He might want to grow his own tomatoes in the garden. That's easy. You can show him how to do that. He might want to know why stones on the beach are a particular shape. If you're a geologist, you're prepared. If not, you may have to get a book from the library, or call in a rock-collecting friend.

Of course, he will never get around to asking about tools if he never sees your husband's workshop, or about pebbles if he never sees a beach. The stimulus must be available.

Heavens, you think, I can't show him the whole world! But a good beginning is to introduce him to the sort of things you yourself like to do. People who read a great deal, for example, will naturally provide books and read stories to their offspring. Accountants may well play counting games with their children. Painters will draw pictures. It is hardly surprising, therefore, that children often (but let me warn you, not always) show talents similar to those of their parents.

Imaginative Play

Many children's games mimic adult activity. This is why little girls play at cooking the dinner or at mothering their dolls, and boys play with hammers or imitate cleaning Daddy's car. All children, fundamentally, want to be grown-ups as quickly as possible, and in imagination they are *being* Mother or Father—not just any mother or father, but their own. Incidentally, don't be disturbed if your child identifies with the opposite sex. It is normal in this age group.

Don't discourage imaginative play, ever. Even if you are told that something has happened that you know very well hasn't really happened, go along with it.

I'll give you an example. My daughter Merle, round about the age of two, was ill in bed with mumps on a gray November day. She was sitting there, looking sick and miserable. Then, as I walked past her bed, she said quite brightly, "Mommy, I'm sitting in the sunshine, and I'm playing with the sand."

"How nice," I said. "Is the sunshine making you very hot?" (She was feverish.) She agreed it was, so I suggested, "Wouldn't you like to take your bed jacket off so that you can sit there and enjoy the sun?"

"Oh yes."

155

So I removed her woolen bed jacket, which made her feel a little cooler and more comfortable; but more important, she had created a situation in her imagination that was enjoyable to replace the miserable situation she was really in. It would have been downright cruel if I hadn't played along and helped her to pretend she *was* sitting in the sun.

But that doesn't apply only to children who are sick; it applies to any child who is playing an imaginative game. Haven't you heard a boy squatting in a grocer's cardboard box tell you that he's driving the fastest car on the track?

If you are asked to join in, join in. Imagination is beneficial, even—if we must use so clinical a word—therapeutic. It is against the interests of your child to learn too soon that the magic and glamour with which he can endow the most ordinary situations are transitory, and that as he grows up he will have to part with these wonders. Don't disenchant his world prematurely. Encourage him to believe in "his car" or "her sandpit" or fairies or Santa Claus. It will make your life richer.

Story-Time

The story that is acted out is infinitely more valuable than the one that is merely read. To start with, of course, you'll have to read it. But forget about your dignity and be that sheep. Say "Baa-baa-baa."

That children like repetition is never so obvious as at story-time. They will ask for the same one over and over, until eventually they know every word by heart. At one point, the child becomes the sheep and says the "baas," and you must be all the other characters. If you have more than one child, the whole thing becomes almost a play-reading.

This is all very exciting and hardly conducive to sleep, you say. Whatever happened to the cozy, nightly bedtime story? In my opinion, it should never have been. These play-readings are not inended for every day, and certainly not for making a child sleepy.

I'm not saying you should never read to a quiet, attentive child. But I am saying it is better to tell your children a story well *before* they go to bed. They are then unable to hang onto you for another five sentences or another page or to the end of the story—and you as an adult have the right to your own free evening. I'm in favor of giving your child a picture book to look at or allowing him to have soft toys in his bed or crib. These are companions. They give a greater feeling of security, which in turn helps him to settle down happily to the idea of being in bed on his own, while you are downstairs.

Playing on His Own

There is no reason why you always have to be ready and available. You won't have a life of your own if you are. Your child will latch on to the idea that you're a sort of ever-ready companion, and that he owns you. He must learn to play by himself, or with the people or creatures he's

157

invented, without your assistance. And you must learn when you can safely (without endangering your relationship with your child) and happily (because you respect each other's rights in this matter) say, "Look, I'll be ready in a little while."

Promising him that you'll come in five minutes or ten minutes doesn't mean anything to a child who can't tell time. He won't understand whether you mean hours or years, but in a "little while" does convey something. "I'll be ready in a little while" will usually satisfy him—provided you have started on the right foot and haven't previously always dropped everything to do his bidding.

Don't decide one bright Tuesday morning, "Ah, the regime from now on is going to be different. I'm not going to be at your beck and call any more." This would make him feel cut off and puzzled, and because you've never behaved like this before, he's going to wonder whether he has made you angry.

As always, it's a question of striking the right balance. If naughtiness can be caused by giving your child too much attention, it can certainly also be caused by the other extreme: ignoring him completely.

You should not expect your child to play contentedly with his toys for hours on end, never needing attention, while you do something complex that requires all your mental concentration. That is the sort of occasion on which you will suddenly notice he's poking in the kitchen cabinet where you keep all your cleaning materials, or turning on the gas, or painting himself with your lipstick.

Very often this kind of mischief is not just the result of

his curiosity about what would happen if he did something or other. He knows that if he does that outrageous thing, you will have to give him some attention.

Thinking back, I can sincerely say that, although I did not have a particularly restrictive regime in my house, I have never had any disastrous accidents, and my house was not one of those that are arranged to be child-proof. I can only put this down to how I always communicated with them, if only at intervals, no matter what I was doing. A child can happily play next to you while you are busy if you spare him a word when he asks you to. You can even say, if you are doing something that requires all your concentration, "Just a minute. Wait now. I'll think about that in a moment." What you must *not* do is ignore him altogether.

I should add that the particularly lively-minded child—and this shows from eighteen months onward—may well need more than the attention you can give him; in other words, he may need the child-oriented environment of a nursery school. I shall talk about this in detail later.

How Much Television?

A word about television. Personally, I think a reasonable amount of viewing can benefit the child under five. It can teach him about things beyond your own family's horizons. It will extend his knowledge and stimulate his imagination, and it's a pleasant pastime to amuse him when the weather

159

keeps him indoors or when he's convalescing from illness.

However, if you let him watch constantly, he'll be in danger of becoming glossy-eyed, much too passive. Watching a puppet dancing on TV calls for far less mental energy than does looking at a picture book and conjuring up its action for yourself. We, as adults, know—don't millions of us watch those televised dramatizations rather than going to the effort of reading the classics on which they are based? Limit your use of television; make it a tool for learning and a treat—not something to keep your child out of mischief all day long.

Incidentally, don't forget that program censorship is your responsibility, not the television network's. It's up to you to decide what your child should see or not see, and to turn the television off before *that show* flashes onto the screen. Of course, your child will look forward to certain favorite programs. That's understandable. Occasionally, watch his programs with him, so that you are able to discuss them together. If you don't, you'll lose an important point of contact.

Gaining His Cooperation

A frequent cause of tension between parents and small children (and, for that matter, parents and older children) is that children are ruthlessly dragged away from games to have a bath, to go out for the day, to come in for a meal.

There should be a rule in the house—a rule imposed by the parents upon themselves—to give notice to a child that, let us say, in ten minutes he will have to stop playing.

Now that you know that play is his "work," you can appreciate how maddening it must be for him to abandon his army or hospital just when he's got it going. A little warning on your part is a courtesy, and should gain for you the cooperation you seek. For this purpose I'd recommend buying a child a cheap watch as soon as he can tell the time, so that he is able to work out when he must be in and end his game accordingly.

True, "ten minutes" doesn't mean much to a child *before* he can tell time. However, if you're consistent about a ten-minute advance-warning system, he'll begin to get the "feel" of how much time he has left. And he'll be more willing to depart from his world for a time and join ours.

23

How to Discipline the

Developing Personality

The subject is discipline. The reason for discipline is that all of us live in relationship to other people—not only the intimate relationship of a household, but also the more general one with close neighbors, and fellow townsmen, and fellow countrymen. We have to draw a line between what we want and what is fair to others, so we have to teach our children to compromise between their own demands and the rights of those among whom they live.

This process begins at the beginning, not suddenly when a child has become so unruly that his parents consider him impossible to handle. When a mother moans, "I can't cope with him," it is too late for her to teach him to:

distinguish between right and wrong; accept rules for everybody's social benefit; respect people and property. Discipline starts when your child's life starts.

Trouble at Bedtime

With the small baby, I have been specific about not letting him cry needlessly, because if he's crying, he wants something: food, his diaper changed, or perhaps just comforting companionship. And I'm not going back on that. Certainly, a baby who needs something should be attended to. But equally, you're allowed a few minutes' grace. You don't have to dash to him the second he opens his mouth, leaving the milk boiling over, or your robe half off. It's good for him to learn to wait a little, while you get things ready.

But suppose there's nothing to get ready? You have just fed him, he's burped, his diaper is dry, he's snugly and smoothly tucked in, he's not too hot or too cold, he doesn't appear to be lonely or frightened . . . AND IT IS TWO O'CLOCK IN THE MORNING! He is simply yelling for the sake of it. Well, tell him so. Say firmly, "There's nothing wrong with you, feller. I'm not going to pick you up, so you might as well go to sleep."

Better still, use Father's magic touch. This is often an occasion when his firm "No" will send the baby off like a lamb while yours has no effect whatever. This is because you, due to your intense emotional relationship with the baby, don't quite mean what you are saying. Secretly, you

163

are thinking, "If he doesn't go to sleep, I suppose I had better pick him up—" And your baby knows it.

Well, Father doesn't mean that at all. Father means: "I'm going back to sleep regardless. I've got to work tomorrow. No means No."

If the baby is just crying for attention, he'll recognize that he can't win, and will settle down. But if he senses a loophole in Mother's attitude, he will wriggle through it, in order to get her where he wants her. And the more often you indulge him, the more often he'll expect to be indulged. So don't hesitate to call on Father for his more determined "No" if you don't quite trust yourself to mean yours.

Bedtime discipline begins when you bring the baby home from the hospital, and it is simply this: once he is in his crib—and that means after the 6 P.M. feeding—whatever further attention he needs (the next feeding, a change of diaper or, later on, a little comfort when he's teething) should be given him in his bedroom. Never, never bring him downstairs again unless the house catches fire. This way, he won't think about that nice exciting living room and cry to be taken there. He'll assume that it's not possible after dark and that his lot is to stay put.

I have known people who've complained about the difficulty of getting their children to go to bed and stay there. Then, when I visit them, I find that they take their baby or toddler out of bed at ten o'clock at night and carry him downstairs to "meet the guest." The baby's petted and fussed over and given a drink, and then he's expected to go to bed again. And they're surprised that he doesn't want to go, and worse, that he asks for the same treatment the next night. Well, I'm surprised only that the parents have any time to themselves at all.

Make two absolutely firm rules: (1) that you will never bring baby downstairs after bedtime, and (2) that you will never, never, never take him into your bed. Yes, even when he's screaming and you're convinced that the extra cuddle and warmth are all he needs to send him off to sleep. If you weaken once, he'll scream every night until you take him in again. And every man and woman have a right to the privacy of their own bed.

As for the infant who needs a night feeding, go into his room and nurse him or give him his bottle there on a chair. Just make sure he's wrapped warmly enough.

Defiance

With every child from about sixteen months old, you will encounter defiance about going to bed. What is wrong with going to bed? Mainly, that he's going there without you. You have to remind yourself that once, not so long ago, he lived in intimate, continuous contact with you, and now there are increasing periods when he's away from you. Isn't he bound to crave your physical closeness? He also imagines that a lot of exciting things are going to happen in the rest of the house the moment he is sent to bed. Tough. But he needs his sleep and you need your evening.

So do not let him prolong the bedtime ritual. As I said earlier, it's inadvisable at this point to undertake acting out

165

a story or other stimulating activities. But that's no reason why you shouldn't invent something to make going to bed appear just a little desirable. Seeing, for example, how quickly both of you can get there, or having a race from bathroom to bedroom. It is something he can look forward to every night, and it has the advantage of hurrying him up.

I'm a great believer in avoiding a problem rather than having to solve one later on. If your child grows up hating or fearing bed, you'll get this sort of dialogue every evening:

"Don't want bed."

"Yes, you do; it's bedtime."

"No!" Tears.

"Come along. Good boy . . ."

"No!" He goes rigid, starts to bawl.

"Yes." You take his hand and pull him upstairs.

"Hate you. Hate you . . ." Exit screaming child.

Very often the more tired the child, the more difficult he is about going to bed. But you must begin the way you intend to continue. If you once stay with him and, let us say, lie down on his bed next to him until he's asleep, don't be surprised if he still expects you to do so when he's eight years old. I have known quite a few mothers in my time whose husbands sat alone for as long as three hours night after night while Mother was desperately trying (a) to creep away from the bed without inciting a riot, or (b) to keep awake as she lay next to the child! Poor lonely Dad down there, denied his right to his wife's companionship. But don't blame the child. Mother started it.

If the child is accustomed from the beginning to being put to bed with whatever small ritual helps him to go happily, then you won't have any serious trouble. Of course, he'll complain and plead. No normal, healthy child wants to stop playing and lie down. The only one I ever knew who regularly said, "I'm tired, Mommy. Can I go to bed?" recently had a rather serious operation. Though your child may not go willingly, he'll go reasonably.

If he feels lonely up there on his own, let him take a Teddy bear or any other favorite companion to bed with him. If he is afraid of the dark, or pretends to be afraid of the dark, I'd suggest a small electric night light. Leaving his door open so that he can see the light shining from the hall and hear distant, comforting noises from downstairs will also help.

But there's a difference between granting requests of this kind and the everlasting drink of water, or the father who when he says goodnight to his son also has to kiss seventeen toy animals all round the room! The latter situation is an extreme example of what not to do, and indeed an example of efficient disciplinary action of child against parent! Such entrapment frustrates you and harms your child, for it teaches him that *you* have to compromise; he doesn't. If he shouts loudly enough and often enough, he wins. And you should be the winner—not because you are bigger but because you are wiser.

Angels with Dirty Hands

No child is good all the time. If you are expecting your first baby, and you nurture a rosy, romantic dream of a contented, gurgling child who grows into a beautiful adult—forget it. There ain't no such animal. The nicest, most easygoing, most loving child will at times be unhappy, tired, frustrated; and quite often you won't even know what he's fretting about. It may be that you have unwittingly mishandled something, or that you handled it admirably but he's misunderstood. Or it may simply be, with a baby between eight months and two years, a case of deliberately violating some household rule to provoke you and thereby obtain attention.

At this age children must be taught what they may and may not do. Have you operated on the premise that almost nothing a child does around the house is intrinsically wrong? Or, does it depend on the value you attach to what he's touching? I'll give you an example. If you own an old sofa that stands in the hall, you probably don't mind when your children jump up and down on it or wheel their muddy toy cars across it. But the Louis XIV settee in the living room, which took you ten years to save for—that's a different story. The children are hardly allowed to look at that without first washing their hands!

Please don't imagine I'm advocating a regime in which the child may treat his home as he pleases; I'm not. Admittedly, a very house-proud mother may well be too restrictive to provide a happy, relaxed atmosphere: her child mustn't lean against the window lest his fingers leave a greasy print; he must always have spotless hands when playing on the cream-colored living room carpet; he mustn't investigate anything that isn't specifically passed to him as a toy, in case he harms it.

168

Our own children were allowed a good deal of freedom around the house, but heaven help them if they had ever torn one of my beloved books or scratched a cherished record of my husband's; both were accessible on low shelves. Our children simply learned that there were certain things they mustn't do.

I realize it's a considerable test for you as a disciplinarian, but I'm positively in favor of leaving such temptations for your child right in the room where he generally plays—the magazine rack, the television knobs (but unplug the TV set, its voltage is deadly), a china ashtray. He'll never learn what No means if everything round him is permissive.

The Meaning of No

Even when he knows what is not permissible, he may do it anyway, to provoke you. Provocative behavior in children from about the age of a year upward can take all sorts of forms.

So your fourteen-month-old knows he shouldn't touch the papers on your desk, but he does, just to annoy you. He may also do something downright dangerous such as reaching into the fire, or he may suddenly hit or bite you or kick your favorite chair, or deliberately knock over the container of milk, and perform any of a hundred other bits of mischief designed surefire to make you mad.

First of all you say "No," and indicate by your tone of

voice and your subsequent behavior that you mean "No." Long before this cranky day, you have made it clear to him that he's not to go near the fire or kick the chair. And when he reaches for the milk container or slaps you, tell him: "Leave the milk alone, John, or you'll spill it," or "Hitting me is rude and unkind. Now stop it."

Your "No" may be sufficient reprimand, but with this age group I am afraid it seldom is. The whole point is that he is in a bad mood and wants to take it out on you.

When Words Fail

What do you do when asking him or telling him fails? If he is reaching for the fire, don't discuss it; distract him with a toy. But when he's just plain being impossible, without endangering himself? Well, this is possibly the only book on the care of children published in the last fifteen years in which the author dares to advise: Smack him. Young children are young animals, and I have never yet trained a puppy or a kitten without the occasional whack. You've tried being reasonable; you've tried being authoritative, and you've failed . . . *and for the sake of your child's entire future you must not fail.* It is part of your responsibility as a parent to teach him discipline.

So give him a sharp slap on the hand, the leg, or bottom, and remove him from the scene so that he won't have a chance to repeat the offense. (This advice works for older children, too. Pride is very dear to a four-year-old, and he may reckon he's got to have the last word, if the target's still within reach.) Putting him to bed, for example, will (a) remove him from the scene of his crime and (b) relieve his tiredness and crankiness.

Now, just let me stress that physical punishment does not mean beating and bruising your child. It doesn't mean slapping his face, boxing his ears, or hitting him with a baseball bat, or any one of the terrible things for which some parents have been sent to jail. But a good swat on the bottom, for doing something anti-social—ill-treating you or his brothers and sisters or a friend or an animal or a bird—will be to his ultimate advantage.

Giving In

Let me warn you that it is usually far, far easier to say "Yes" than "No." And some days, often when a child is fed up with his toys, everything seems to him to be a "no-no." First he pulls at a pile of papers on the writing desk. "Stop that, Antony," you say.

He bashes on the French window with a spoon. "Antony, no."

He kicks at the gate across the stairs. "No."

He goes back to the papers again, and you think, "Perhaps it wouldn't matter if I let him play with just that one. After all, it is only a circular, and I've already read it . . ."

COMMON SENSE IN CHILD REARING

"All right, Antony, just that one," you say. "Oh, if you must—Aunt Amy's letter, too, but no more . . ."

I'm willing to bet that at bedtime you will be gathering up the entire pile of papers, all of them messed up or torn, including the phone bill and the bank statement.

And your child will have learned a lesson: Mother doesn't mean "No"—not if you push her long enough.

And you should have meant "No" because, after all, you needed the phone bill and the bank statement intact. If those papers had all been old circulars and your child had wanted to play with them, it would have been all right to let him. But if you're going to say "yes," say "yes" from the start.

Whenever your child makes a request, consider first whether it is reasonable and whether you can grant it. I'll give you an example where a mother might be tempted to refuse. A twenty-month-old boy says, for instance, "Jumbo. Want Jumbo."

"No, not now," says Mother, because spongy Jumbo is upstairs in a closet and she doesn't want to be bothered fetching it. Child begins to fret, and Mother tries to distract him with other toys. Child gets cross and shouts repeatedly for Jumbo. Mother realizes it will take less time and energy to climb the stairs and fish out Jumbo than to play here with her son in an attempt to appease him. So she complies and is rewarded with peace.

But, once again, child has learned a lesson: If you want a thing, keep whining for it and eventually Mother will give in. All too soon this principle is extended from a reasonable request to an annoying one such as wanting drinks of water all day long, and then to something intolerable such as picking the prize dahlias in the park.

I was in the bakery the other day when a mother came in with her two-year-old, who was clutching a dripping popsicle.

"Cakie!" demanded the little girl, pointing to a Viennese pastry.

"No, darling," her mother said, "you've got a popsicle and you had some chocolate before that."

"Cakie!" shouted Darling.

Mother paid for the bread she'd come for, and by now her daughter was screaming. "And one of those cream cakes," Mother added resignedly to the girl behind the counter.

I swear to Heaven I didn't say a word but my shock must have shown in my face, because the mother turned to me and said, "I have to give in to her. If I don't she screams. She's got a demanding nature, you see."

I saw, all right. Here was a mother who had never said "No" and truly meant it. And she excused her own weakness, her failure, by blaming her child's "demanding nature." I will admit that there are a few children whose genes create a tendency in them to be mean, unstable and violent. But I firmly believe that the vast majority of selfish, unpleasant, demanding children would have been perfectly acceptable little people if only their parents had disciplined them correctly. That child in the bakery had a "demanding nature" because she'd learned that if "Darling" demanded loudly enough, what "Darling" wanted, "Darling" got.

24

The Perverse Age

Just when you think you've got young Timothy to the stage when you can say "Bedtime in ten minutes," and he'll groan but start parking cars in his garage, he will turn round and say, "Not bedtime!" Eighteen months to two years is a perverse age during which children will oppose everything. Whatever you suggest—no, they want to do something else.

A mother might say to her twenty-one-month old little girl, "Would you like to put your red dress on?"

"No. Don't want my red dress!" Mother is puzzled because she knows her daughter likes the dress.

"Which dress would you like to put on?"

In fact the little girl doesn't want to put on any dress, because she's just being Mary, Mary quite contrary. It's a phase. If you handle it correctly, she'll have outgrown it by the time she goes to school. If you haven't, she will be telling you what dress *you* are to wear!

So as soon as you recognize that your child has entered the contradicting phase, don't suggest. Instead, tell. "Today we're going to put on the red dress. We are now going out for a walk. The sun is lovely and we're going shopping." Don't ask, "Would you like to?"

The phase will pass much faster if the child can't play boss; if she can't dumbfound you by replying, "No, I don't want to go shopping." Actually, you see, what she is doing is pitting her will against yours to see who's going to be boss.

And, believe me, in her heart of hearts she wants you to tell her what to do. She wants the security of knowing you have the strength to make the decisions; to find this out, she has to test you. So you indicate to her, without any clash, that you do have the strength. If you don't, you're not strong enough to be a parent.

Sadly, too many children under five have already learned that their mothers and fathers are not equipped to be parents. This is pathetic, because the parent who is weak nevertheless has experience, and the child who is so much stronger nevertheless hasn't. The result, of course, is chaos. The child cannot handle himself; he is unable to teach himself, and there is no one to help him.

Losing Your Temper

By the time your child has passed the two-year mark, his misdemeanors will probably annoy you far more. You're aware that he knows perfectly well what he's doing, and yet he defies you. I know how easy it is to lose your temper when the little beast tips red paint over your white curtains, or perhaps has banged a door you've twice asked him to close. Under the stress of emotion unconnected with his "crime"—your money worries, family problems, health— you overpunish. Instead of administering a judicious slap, you angrily whack, whack, whack—yelling at him all the while.

Then, having done so and thereby relieved your own feelings, you think, "Oh, Lord, what have I done! My poor child!" All right, think it but don't do anything about it, not then. Don't take him into your arms and, as it were, negate by verbal comfort whatever usefulness might have come out of your having indicated your disapproval so violently. Instead, when you feel more reasonable and when the child has calmed down, apologize. "Look, I'm sorry I had to hit you so hard, but what you did was rather awful."

The child will remember the smarting bottom and the effectiveness of your king-sized punishment won't have been lost for the future; and such an apology on your part will assure him that you didn't hurt him because you hate him. Your love is still his. You simply lost your temper.

Children have an innate sense of justice. They almost never resent retribution; it is only the unjust punishment

176

that festers. So, let him see why he made you angry and he'll accept philosophically that the extra swats resulted from his bad timing.

The Tantrum

It is generally true that the child who harbors violent emotions will not be helped if we match our emotions to his. I am thinking here particularly of the child who is given to tantrums. Slapping him and shouting at him in the middle of his tantrum is merely going to cause a clash between your temper and his. It isn't an application of discipline. It may be an outlet for you, but that isn't the object, is it?

The correct way to deal with a tantrum is to keep calm and to remove the child from the place where it occurs. Preferably get him alone with you, not surrounded by worried, frightened, perhaps overindulgent grandparents and friends whose reaction unconsciously encourages a scene. In a quiet atmosphere, your child will cool down faster.

I know. I have a daughter of my own who is given to intense emotions and opinions, and when she was little she suffered—rather, the whole family suffered—from her violent tantrums. At times she got so pent-up with frustration, because the world frequently had the audacity to go its own way instead of hers, that there was sometimes a real danger that she would attack her brother or sister, us or friends, or

177

even do herself some injury. With all this suppressed emotion bubbling under the surface, she was certainly not a pleasant person to have around. I was forever carting her off into empty rooms and talking to her calmly. I got fed up with it.

Then, one day I decided to sacrifice a large cushion, the largest we had, in the interest of peace. It was bright orange and stuffed with bits of foam rubber. She went into one of her tantrums and, thus prepared, I took her into her bedroom, gave her the cushion, and said to her, "Now, I don't care what you do to this, but you do it in here alone. When you feel fit to rejoin the human race, you can come out again." I gave her the freedom to decide for herself when she was over what had made her so uptight.

I don't know what she did to the cushion on the first occasion. There was a great deal of noise in there, but I kept away. When she reappeared twenty minutes later, she looked quite different, obviously happier, and joined in with whatever the family was doing. We behaved as though she'd just come in from the yard—no inquests, no scoldings.

For the next few years, we used the cushion, or I should say *she* used the cushion, because its use became a voluntary act whenever she felt a tantrum coming on. It got to the point where one day she said, with barely suppressed tears, "I'm going to see my hate cushion," and that became its nickname: the hate cushion.

If you're wondering what on earth she did to it, you'll sympathize with my own curiosity. One day I peeped through the door and there she was, doing just about everything you can imagine to her cushion—she bit it; she pummeled it; she kicked it; she threw it; she buried her head in it. But she got rid of that excess of fury.

You may well ask how did I know it would work. Perhaps the simplest answer to that is that I am a person of violent emotions myself. There have been many occasions when scrubbing a floor or beating a carpet or savagely sweeping the walk has relieved my feelings. It used up my angry energy.

But I couldn't get a two-and-a-half-year-old to scrub the floor or beat a carpet, so I hit upon the cushion idea. But I knew instinctively that it had to be a private confrontation. She had to be helped to help *herself* control those strong feelings. I feel sure that if one controls a child so that he doesn't show his feelings, one will merely suppress them, not eradicate them. They'll only come out in some other, probably less desirable way.

Bedtime Ruses

In the age group from two to three and a half, you will get the runaround at bedtime. He's not such a little thing anymore; he's not drowsy enough to close his eyes. So he looks about and plots schemes for summoning his mother. A drink of water is always a good beginning. Don't fall for it. He doesn't want a drink, though he may force down the one you bring him—he wants you upstairs. A neat way of combatting the young child who claims to be "dying of thirst" is to offer him a drink of water just before bedtime. That way you know any genuine thirst has been satisfied. (The drawback to this is that you may create a wet diaper problem. Choose your lesser evil.)

"Mommy, I've got a secret to tell you . . ." "I want to kiss Daddy goodnight . . ." "Mommy, my—er—er—head hurts . . ." Oh, there are lots of fine reasons for you to go to him, and not one of them will be valid.

Once he's in a bed, of course, he can get out and come down to you. They know how to look so appealing in the nightclothes, clutching Teddy and standing in the doorway. Daddy especially may well be seduced by his little girl's smile and reach out to cuddle her. But I advise you to march infant straight upstairs again without so much as a Hello.

In the case of a normal, healthy child, I cannot think of anything that would require you to talk to him again before morning—regardless of visitations, calls, demands for this, that, or the other.

If you go upstairs because your child has shouted for a drink of water four times and instead of giving him that drink you slap him, don't assume that you have applied the right disciplinary measure. You haven't. Although you've slapped him, you've also gone upstairs and given him attention, which is what he really wanted, and as far as he's concerned, bad attention is better than no attention at all.

If, on the other hand, your child is really ill, say with earache or measles, then naturally he will need your comforting presence. He may well feel fretful and be unable to sleep because he's uncomfortable and feverish. So when he calls or cries, you must, of course, answer.

180

The same applies to a child who is disturbed. He will wake screaming with terror from a dream, in genuine distress. Don't say in this case, "There's nothing he could possibly want; let's leave him to scream."

But be careful during a sick child's convalescence to withdraw your constant companionship. Otherwise you will still be running upstairs perhaps fifteen times a night when he's ten and saying, "You know, he was fine until he was three, but then he got the measles and ever since then he can't sleep and I have to go to him . . ."

25

Lies, Obscenity, and

Misbehavior in Public

Most three-year-olds tell whoppers. Now, when we consider lying, and what disciplinary action we should take against it, we must clearly differentiate between the child who is creating fantasy, the child who lies to get himself out of possible trouble, and the child who is chronically unable to come to terms with reality—and children in that last category, who are in a very small minority, need expert help, not punishment.

We have already discussed fantasy in play—for example, the child who makes believe a cardboard box is a racing car. At one time or another he may suddenly come out with: "I am the King of Africa." Don't worry, your small son is not suffering from delusions; he's perfectly aware he's not really. You don't have to point it out. As long as it is tacitly understood by both you and your child that this is a tall story, a bit of fun, a game, play along.

My children and I have told tall stories quite deliberately, sometimes just to see how tall they could get. My middle daughter, the one with the tantrums and the superb imagination, frequently amused ladies on buses by telling them that she was a Martian in disguise. Personally, I don't think this sort of thing does any harm, provided everyone agrees that this is a game that the family is playing for a specific time only.

So that leaves the middle category, the child who lies to get himself out of trouble. Heinous crime, you say. Well, you'd just better be sure he never catches you falsely telling an acquaintance you're so sorry you can't attend the PTA dinner because you have a previous engagement. "You lied, Mommy," he'll say, shattered.

Anyway, let's assume that tricky situation won't occur. First of all, you need to be sure that your child *is* lying. You must learn to understand the tone of his voice, his attitude, the whole of his behavior when he is accused of telling a lie, so that you can be sure of the facts. He's innocent until proven guilty . . . although he may confess later!

Well, if you can persuade him to admit finally that indeed he did do whatever it was, and that he lied to cover it up, it might just be worthwhile on this occasion to spare him from the original punishment as a reward for owning up. If he never owns up, but shamelessly continues to blame

183

his sister or his playmate or the cat, and you have *proof* that he is lying, then give him a double punishment—half for the deed and half for the lie.

Discipline in Public

Discipline inevitably involves punishment—for instance, I've just mentioned a double punishment for lying. But how should you punish? We've already discussed reprimands for a first offense and slaps for subsequent offenses. Trouble is, it isn't always convenient to smack your child. For example, you're out shopping in a busy street. The child is bored, tired, and cranky, and he provokes you. Apart from not wanting to sacrifice your composure by physically clashing with him, it would be unfair to him. Public humiliation involves a loss of face, way out of proportion in his eyes to the size of his misdemeanor.

This is equally true of a crowded room at home. If Father, Grandma, and particularly his friends or brothers and sisters are present, it's much better to take your young delinquent away and administer the slap out of their sight and earshot.

But going back to the street . . . there you don't have the chance to take him elsewhere, and to hit him two hours afterward, when you're home again, strikes me as almost sadistic. So what are the alternatives? You can withdraw extra privileges—ice cream that you were going to buy when you passed the Good Humor truck, for example; or a special outing he was looking forward to, like a visit to the zoo.

You will have to bear in mind that he might not be the only one looking forward to it! And having once said, even in a temper, "All right. You were naughty. You can't go to the zoo on Sunday," you'll have to stick to it. And even if Sunday is bright and sunny and the whole family is itching for that day out, you'll have to settle for a walk in the park. No matter how much you realize that it was a dumb thing to have said, if you dare to go back on it your child will know for all time that your threats are empty ones.

For the child in a temper, sitting him somewhere until you tell him he can stand is a punishment with a calming effect. But you may have to order him back there several times, because *he* must not be allowed to decide when he's served his sentence. On the other hand, don't go away to put the laundry in the washing machine and forget all about him. For other children, like my daughter, it works better if you do let her be the judge. You can say, for example, "You stay in your room until you think you are capable of coming out."

But locking a child in a room is never, never, never justified. Whatever he's done, this is still his home, not a prison. To withdraw food from him is also wrong. The old Victorian "You go to bed without your supper" belongs only in fairy tales and old novels. Equally, "I won't love you—if you do that, Mommy can't love you" is a cruel thing to say to a child. You should love him always, and he should know it—even when you have to smack him.

Strangely enough, children are well aware that those who apply discipline correctly do so because they love them. Children know that they need firm handling. Not only do small children know this, but teen-agers are aware of it, too. Very often the outrageous things they do are a bid to make their parents care about them enough to stop them. One of the saddest comments I ever heard was when a young girl told me, "My school isn't making me work hard enough." She knew she was not yet able to apply the required discipline to herself, and yet nobody else seemed interested enough to do it for her.

Children accept that they need to be told what to do. They even accept that they need to be punished for failing to do it. Therefore they respect those who apply discipline correctly and have contempt for those who don't. So be a parent your child can love and admire, not despise.

Obscenity

For all parents of under-fives, the day dawns when they hear their child swear. Though you will immediately feel obliged to put a stop to it, you will not stop it by opposing it. Punish your child for swearing and he will surely swear forever. No, there is a tried and tested method for curing swearing children, the same method I apply on the adult upstarts who hurl obscene language at me. I do nothing; I ignore it. Very soon the swearer wearies of using his explosive phrases when I don't seem to notice them. And

186

they were meant to shock me. He'd learned them specifically for that purpose. The swearing phase in a child will pass with similar disillusionment.

I carried out this routine with my own three children, one after the other. The end result is that none of my children swears. The only person in our household who still swears is me—probably because years and years ago my ladylike mother was so satisfyingly horror-stricken!

The number of times you will have to apply discipline will largely depend on your child's temperament and your own, and the extent to which you have a friendly, human relationship rather than a parent-child one. The more you will use real consideration and courtesy toward your child in speech and action, the less often will situations arise that call for firm disciplinary measures.

Certainly I agree that your child must learn to obey you. But in turn you should honor him—and that means having respect for his rights and his feelings. And, most important, you should love him at all times—even when he fails and disappoints you.

Playing Off the Parents

Now, it's not much good if one parent is fair and the other parent spoils the child at every turn. If you expect your punishments to be effective, you must always present a united front before the child. Of course, you may say later—in a private and calm discussion, not a row that

187

resounds through the house so that your child knows you didn't agree about it—that you didn't think such-and-such a punishment suited the misdeed. You can come to some mutual, satisfactory arrangement for future occasions. But in front of the child you must present an unyielding, shoulder-to-shoulder front line.

You must never allow a situation to arise where your child knows he can play one of you off against the other. As a little girl, I discovered only too soon that I could play my mother off against my father and vice versa, and I managed to carve out a pretty good life for myself over many years. In fact, I got them to the point where they unconsciously encouraged me! When I persuaded my father to let me do something I knew my mother disapproved of, he'd wink at me and say, "All right, but don't tell your mother!" The converse was also true. My parents, I am sorry to say, are textbook examples of poor disciplinarians.

26

How to Choose a Sitter

If your child is to grow into an independent adult, he must be encouraged in infancy to take a few steps away from the apron strings, toward people besides his parents. There are going to be occasions when you simply have to go somewhere and it is impossible to take him along; and other occasions when you just don't want him along.

You'll be condemning yourself to a grim future if you decide that never again can you and your husband go out in the evenings, never can you browse through the downtown shops of an afternoon, never ever can you plan anything that doesn't include your child.

Of course, *no small child should ever be left alone in*

the house—even for a short time, and even if he is safely asleep in his crib.

Like everything else we have so far considered, your child's adjustment from total dependence on you to an acceptance of your absence, and the presence of someone else, has to be *gradual*. You must not be available every second for months and then, because he has been weaned and can walk, suddenly decide, "All right, now Mrs. X. can look after him." If you do, the shock of finding himself suddenly bereft of the figure of love and comfort he knows may affect him emotionally, deeply and bitterly. He needs to learn slowly and gently that others can be trusted, and that Mother always comes back to him.

After all, the daily loss of Father from eight in the morning till six at night, or whatever, makes him unhappy, but the fact that Father reappears just before Baby's bedtime reassures him and gradually accustoms him to such a routine. (I am aware that there are many situations in which this cannot happen—a husband may well return home long after his child's bedtime, or he may have to be away for weeks on end. I am merely creating the ideal.)

Father's presence is of almost as much importance as Mother's. This is well-known to welfare workers, probation officers, and others who are concerned with the care of young people: the continuous absence of fathers in World War II increased the percentage of teen-age delinquents, who seemed to need to hit back at the world. In the main, those fathers were absent during their children's babyhood and early infancy, not the later years.

The First Evening Away

I have often reminded you that mothers should not forget that they are wives, too. Certainly within the first three weeks after Baby is born, it is desirable that one evening be set aside for husband and wife to go out together, if only to the movies or to visit friends.

Now, although this may sound tempting when you arrange it, at the moment of departure you may develop qualms. After all, the other half of that umbilical cord was joined to you. You think about that warm, soft little body crying for you, and you start taking off your coat. Well, button it up again and GO. He'll be all right—providing, of course, the baby-sitter is trustworthy.

On this first occasion, I would recommend you choose someone you *feel* you can trust, not just someone "who's bound to be all right because she's taken First Aid and everything." Your own mother, or a neighbor who has three children of her own and has already helped you change Baby's diapers, would be ideal.

So you see the movie, overcome the urge to phone home every half-hour, and yet when you get back the sitter reports that the baby was fretful, and cried for his feeding earlier than you said he could have it. You feel guilty about having left him. Don't be. This is normal. What babies don't understand intellectually, they are able to sense, and this was the first big break with Mother. She wasn't even in the house, her presence was nowhere to be felt. Comfort him (if he is still protesting) and a week or so later repeat the

191

process. It won't be long before you are able to go out comfortably for an afternoon, even a whole day.

If your baby refuses to allow you longer than an hour (he doesn't just fret, he positively screams), or you as a mother find the very idea of leaving your child in someone else's hands too painful to contemplate, I advise you to try this. Invite someone for lunch who is good with children, and deliberately go off into the kitchen to get it, leaving this person in the living room to entertain your child. Choose a time when the child is awake—perhaps just before or just after a feeding, so that they will have an opportunity to form a real relationship.

It's good for Baby to get to know other people. It's the first stage in being able to face the world without you, and it is also good for you.

A possessive mother makes for an unhappy child. Possessive mothers start out genuinely believing they are indispensable to their babies, and then proceed to make this true by jealously preventing anyone else from getting close to them—including, in extreme cases, Father. "My child," they say, as if their husband didn't have anything to do with it.

So if you find yourself thinking that nobody else quite knows how to treat your baby, call for a sitter—quick.

Incidentally, it is almost as bad if your baby is tied emotionally to only one other person besides yourself, say his grandmother. Ideally he should have a small circle of people—relatives or friends, whom he will stay with happily. His friends need not be close friends of yours. The seventeen-year-old daughter of the family that lives across the street may be ill at ease with you (perhaps because you are "over thirty"), but she could turn out to be wonderful with your child. And your husband's Aunt Ada may come into her own at last. Her attitude toward babies may not be yours. She may coo baby talk, she may dotingly hold him as long as he wants, she may fasten diapers differently. But as long as your baby likes her and she is a responsible person, it doesn't matter. He'll welcome the change of pace and the rare indulgence.

I say "rare" because I am assuming you will be using Aunt Ada or the girl across the street for comparatively short sessions. If you're thinking in terms of a vacation, someone whose routine and attitude are similar to yours would be infinitely preferable, and someone from his circle whom he knows very well indeed would be the best choice of all.

How About a Vacation?

Because I am so firmly convinced of the importance of maintaining and strengthening not only the parent-child relationship but also the husband-wife relationship, I'm all for short vacations away from your baby. But short is the operative word. Most young mothers wouldn't enjoy a long vacation away from their babies, anyway, so it's not really practical to talk about a month.

Even a week can seem like an eternity to an eight-month-old. However kind and loving the person is who takes care of your baby, she is not you. As far as the baby is concerned, a week might as well be forever. Time is a meaningless concept at this age. The baby has no idea of the future and only a sketchy memory of the past. The present is everything, and at present you are absent.

So at this stage it would probably be a question of just a weekend away. By the time he is a year old, you could safely lengthen this to a week. But even if you are going to leave your child with another person for just a day, it is desirable that he become reacquainted with this person at least a day beforehand.

It also helps if the baby-sitter comes to your house, rather than Baby going to hers. This way at least his room, his crib, the wallpaper, the routine, remain the same. Only the person who looks after him is different.

This approach will especially help the baby who needs to be weaned away from you more gently than you had anticipated—the one who yells every time his carriage is parked in a strange yard. Take it one step at a time: first a friend to talk to while you're out of the room, later a baby-sitter in his house, and finally his acceptance of your "day out."

No Baby-Sitter

If you don't have an Aunt Ada, or a girl across the street, and both sets of grandparents live too far away—in short, you don't have *anyone* to baby-sit, let alone a circle of baby-sitters, I sympathize. Let's try to resolve your problem.

Have you seen anybody at all on your street with young children—not necessarily of the same age as your own baby? If so, approach her and see if you can't come to a reciprocal baby-sitting arrangement. But do be sure it is reciprocal. There is a vast difference between keeping an eye on a baby sleeping in his carriage while his mother goes shopping, and in return entertaining three rowdy youngsters while their mother goes shopping.

At night, for a family who have three children of their own, supervising an extra baby in the house obviously involves little extra responsibility and, provided he doesn't wake, no extra work at all. But to expect that baby's parents to have three children lying on various spare mattresses for an evening is hardly equal return. Some other form of payment would have to be worked out. If it isn't, the system will, I assure you, come to a fast and unhappy end.

Some people I know resort to installing an intercom, with a microphone next to the baby's crib and a speaker in the house next door so that the neighbors can hear the baby if he cries. It's convenient, but frankly I am not happy about it. You can't smell smoke or see sparks through a loud-speaker.

A free, reliable way of getting baby-sitters is to join a baby-sitting circle. If you live in a new housing project, where there are a lot of young families, there is probably one in existence already. If there isn't, start one. Ask at the office for the names and addresses of other mothers with babies and small children who live close to you. Then, get busy with an availability list and a points system—usually

195

one point an hour and two points for sitters after midnight.

The trouble with such circles, however, is that in order to be fair, the circles tend toward the bureaucratic. I've known many parents to drop out because they couldn't stand the fiddling about with half-points for the odd twenty minutes. So try to be patient and see all the paperwork as a necessary evil: it does prevent someone sailing in at 2:00 A.M. from what should have been a few hours at the movies with the bland explanation that "they went on somewhere"!

The Professional Sitter

Now a word, as the radio commercials say, about the professional baby-sitter who advertises on the bulletin board in the supermarket or in the local paper. Usually these are elderly women, who enjoy getting out of their houses and knitting by your fireside or watching your television for a change, or teen-agers who need some peace to do their homework. But make no mistake: both groups do it for money.

So first of all, find out what the standard rate is. It will probably depend on local supply and demand, on whether it's a weekend, on how much work is involved (it will cost more if the children need a meal cooked for them than if they are in bed asleep), and whether the sitter will have to stay after midnight. You should expect, too, to give her some sort of supper. It doesn't have to be filet mignon, but it must be adequate and there must be enough milk, etc., for several cups of coffee, or a couple of glasses of milk, especially for a teen-ager.

My own two daughters have done a fair amount of professional baby-sitting, so I am quite an expert on what one should and shouldn't do to the sitter. My younger daughter once took care of a baby in whose home she discovered there was only about a quarter of a pint of milk and only one diaper—and that after much searching. So please make sure your baby-sitter knows precisely where all the things are that she might need for the baby's comfort and her own.

Remember to show your baby-sitter how to operate your TV set, thermostat, electrical appliances for the kitchen, the lights in the toilet and on the stairs, etc. Allow yourselves an extra ten minutes to explain these things before departing, because it is unsafe to leave someone to grope around in half-darkness searching for something she needs that very moment. (One set of parents actually requested my daughter not to sit with the light on unless she was reading, in order to keep the electricity bill down!)

And while you're preparing to go, be sure to inform the sitter of the household rules—one story only before sleep, or Teddy in bed and not the whole barnyard. And be sure, too, the child knows them. It is not fair to leave a baby-sitter with children who are barely controllable by their own parents, because it is always much more difficult for a stranger to impose discipline.

Arrange to get the sitter home—you can't simply

return at midnight and say, "Here's what we owe you. Thank you very much. Goodnight," and let your sitter walk back.

I've perhaps implied that baby-sitters are an abused lot. On the whole, they're not. They get a free meal and a few extra dollars usually for doing absolutely nothing, while the baby sleeps.

But they are, after all, somewhat like the pilot of a jet plane flying on automatic controls—he's paid to be there for the rare emergency. Be certain that if an emergency arises, the sitter can handle it.

Try to meet her before the big day and make up your own mind that she's capable and trustworthy and that the baby will be happy with her. If she turns out to be a deaf old lady who is wobbly on the stairs and couldn't lift Baby if she had to and wouldn't hear him if he cried, have the courage to apologize and tell her she's not really what you're looking for. After all, we could be talking about your child's life. The same applies to a fifteen-year-old girl who is only interested in a place to neck with her boyfriend. Say no.

Obviously all the rules of good behavior should be extended by parents just as much to the unpaid sitter (the relative or friend or member of the sitting circle).

Finally, be sure you know when *not* to trust. I have some amusing, sophisticated friends whose company I enjoy very much, yet I wouldn't trust them for five minutes in charge of a young child. They wouldn't notice that the child they were supposed to be keeping an eye on had crawled out into the hall and was currently tumbling down the stairs. Don't be ashamed to admit to yourself that some of your friends just don't have the right experience for the job.

27

Preparing an Infant

for a Hospital Stay

So far I have dealt with occasions when you have to leave your baby. It is sad, but a few babies have to leave their parents to go into the hospital. Because there is more you can do to prepare older children for the experience, and because it is then more common, I am going to deal with this problem later. But even one-year-olds understand far more than they can ever say; so talking comfortably in his presence about some key words like "nurse" may help, and an extra dose of love beforehand may sustain him. A withdrawal of love, on the grounds that he's going to be without you for a week or two, certainly won't.

By this time, anyway, your baby is an old hand with

doctors, nurses, vaccination, and inoculations. Nurses, often because they are busy, will take your baby into another room to give him his injection and leave you in the waiting room. Your child won't like the momentary pain of the needle, whatever you do; but if you insist that you hold him while he is being subjected to this necessary discomfort, his emotional pain will be far less. You see, if you stay there (and it's an important thing to keep in mind), at least you haven't abandoned him to suffer pain; you remained with him while it hurt, and it's good for a baby to know he has a mother for better and for worse.

Parting Is Not Sweet Sorrow

When a child between fifteen months and three years of age has to go into a hospital, first of all, make sure that a parting is indeed unavoidable. Because a child needs his mother even more when he's ill or frightened, some enlightened hospitals provide facilities for mothers to sleep there with their children. Mother's comfort at such a time is immeasurable; so if your child is taken to a hospital that permits this—and providing the rest of your family can manage without you for a few days—take advantage of the arrangement.

Unfortunately, not all hospitals have the room—or the enlightened attitude—to allow this yet. But, in a change from the past, most hospitals do permit you to visit your sick child. Once upon a time it was felt that parents upset their

201

children because when visiting hour was over and they had to leave, the children screamed and protested. If they never saw their parents at all during their stay in the hospital, the theory was, they would be quiet and well-behaved—that is, seemingly calm and acquiescent.

Nothing could be further from the truth. Yes, they were quiet enough, perhaps, but what the child suffered secretly by not seeing his parents for perhaps a week, a fortnight, three months, cannot be assessed. There just isn't a scale by which to measure such emotional damage.

Of course, it hurts to wave goodbye to someone you love; even adults cry, so no wonder small children do. But it hurts far, far more to have to assume that this loved one has forgotten your very existence, doesn't it? So, see your child as often as you possibly can, and on days when you cannot get to the hospital, find out if someone like Grandma is able to go instead. It's lonely and humiliating sitting in your crib or bed with no one to talk to, when all the other children are surrounded by Mommies and Daddies. And when you are there, hold back any tears or lumps in the throat until you're outside. A sure-fire way to distress your child is to show your own distress.

And if you are informed that this particular hospital believes children are managed more easily if they are not disturbed by visits from home, tell them that while this may be so, you're not risking the ghastly consequences!

When You're in the Hospital

Before we leave the subject of partings due to hospitalization, I'd like to mention the converse—when *you* have to go into the hospital. In maternity wards I noticed that "first mothers" were usually only too glad to lie back and let the experts take charge of their new arrivals, whereas the women who had children at home were itching to get there within twenty-four hours. They always said they missed their three-year-old or their twins. Their husbands they still saw, albeit briefly, every evening.

For sound reasons, most hospitals forbid junior visitors, and this is tough on both mother and child. I remember one husband telling his wife (rather foolishly) that their four-year-old had stormed that he hated Mommy and never wanted to see her again. What the child really meant was that the separation had been too long for him to cope with. It would do wonders if an ambulatory mother could talk to her child on a terrace or somewhere in the hospital.

28

Leaving Baby Behind

on Vacation

I'd like to turn now to happier reasons for being parted—vacations, for instance. By the time your child is eighteen months old, I hope that he will let you go away for a week and, a year later, for two weeks. But he could be of a highly nervous temperament and, no matter what you do, refuse to allow you out of his sight even for a single afternoon.

If the baby-sitter reports that he screamed the entire time you were gone, make sure first that he didn't cry for any other reason—because of indigestion, because he had a cold coming on, because he was cutting a tooth. Then, if you're certain he's indeed all right, you'll have to work on him. Create brief partings, from a half an hour up, even when they are not imperative; leave him with someone while you do the weekend shopping, even though you could take him in his carriage. It will prepare him to accept separation when it is imperative.

During this period of education, take care that the person who stays with him is not only familiar, kind, and very patient, but confident of her ability to take care of him. If he senses that she has doubts, his own fears will quickly surface. When you return, greet him happily and calmly, even if he is screaming. Comfort him, but be firm. Get across to him the point that he's got his mother back and nothing dreadful has happened in the meantime. Believe me, soon he will start to trust you not to abandon him forever, and in turn he'll find out that the company of other people can even have its advantages.

Hasty Exits

Incidentally, whenever you hand your child over to someone else, try not to dash off instantly. It is a bit bewildering for a child to be dumped on a strange carpet and watch Mommy fly out the door. If you can delay that change-over for five minutes or so, your child will have had time to recall that the new lady in charge is Aunt Meg, and that even if the carpet's strange, his own blocks are sitting in the middle of it.

I am strongly against backing out quietly. Not only is it anti-social (and therefore sets a bad example), but it also causes alarm when he does look up and miss you some twenty minutes later. If you are weaning him away from total dependence on you gradually enough, you should never meet a situation where you have to retreat out the back door while your child is banging on the front one!

So, say goodbye, tell him you're going to buy a pretty new dress and you'll see him for supper. And if he barely glances up in response, good. You can think about that week's vacation.

If you do go away without your toddler, you may find that this older child—unlike the baby, who prefers the routine and surroundings he knows—would welcome a change: a bit of a holiday of his own. He might like living by the sea with Grandma or in the country with Aunt Annie. But the object of his going there is convenience for the sitter and pleasure for him, not to get him away from anything that might remind him of his parents. There is no reason to suppose that forgetting he has parents will benefit any child. Quite the reverse: the lesson to be learned is that he does have a mother and a father, and that the three of them can still love one another even though they're not together.

Reminders of You

It may sound callous, but in my opinion it is even worth a small scene to refresh your child's memory about Mommy and Daddy, because it reassures him that they are around somewhere and that they care about him.

For this reason I'd send him a couple of postcards. He'll look at the pictures, but don't expect your message to have the same value that it would to an eight-year-old. Even when it is explained to him that "This is from Mommy and Daddy, and they send you lots and lots of love and kisses, and they'll be back soon," the child cannot understand intellectually what this means. Yet he can understand emotionally. He will hear the cheerfulness in Grandma's voice as she mentions Mommy and Daddy, and, on a nonverbal level, he will be reassured that all is well.

Remember back to when you were in the flush of your first love and how you used to sit quietly and repeat his name over and over to yourself. Just saying the name or hearing somebody else mention him gave you a feeling of warmth and love, because the sound evoked certain associations. The same thing applies to a young child. There is an ambience of security, love, and happiness to him about the words "Mommy" and "Daddy."

Why He Shouldn't Go with You

After much thought, I've concluded that on the whole I'm against taking a baby on a vacation. We're back to the same old song: babies like routine. Unlike us, they do not long for a change of scene and the chance to meet new people. So the idea of an annual "break" is meaningless to them. I admit the baby over a year might have fun playing on a sandy beach or dipping a foot into a warm lake, with

Mommy and Daddy nearby—assuming, of course, the weather is glorious. But if it rains, staying in a summer cottage or a resort hotel room and coping with a bored baby (because most of his playthings have had to be left behind) is murder.

And I strongly advise you against taking your baby abroad. Even adult travelers get the "trots" or "Montezuma's revenge," as it's called in Mexico. And gastric troubles and sunstroke can be serious in a baby. Besides, even if your travel agent offers you a bargain in a rentable villa in Italy, a chateau in France, or a condominium apartment in Spain, think of all the stuff you'd have to lug: bottles of sterilizing solutions, powdered milk (the foreign milk may not be pasteurized), two dozen cloth diapers (and no guarantee of a laundromat or a washing machine at your destination) or a suitcase full of disposables, and cans and cans and cans of baby food.

In your own home he is surrounded by equipment. Leave his high chair behind and you'll discover how difficult it is to feed a ten-month-old on your lap. Leave his playpen, and you can't turn your back for two minutes. Leave his carriage, and he'll have to walk or be carried everywhere. Leave his crib, and you'll have to rent or borrow one.

And this is true of vacations in this country too. Unless you drive a retired Greyhound bus, you can't take everything. We're so spoiled and so dependent on hot running water and ultra-modern cooking and washing facilities in caring for our babies that I don't recommend camping.

Now if you're about to argue that hotels have high chairs and cribs and private baths with every room, and they do the cooking for you, I agree. They do. But, boy, I think you'll regret it if you take your baby to a hotel. To start with, as I've said earlier in this book, few children under two are socially fit to eat with strangers. So if you have a thought for your fellow guests—and for your baby, who's doing his best (which is good enough for home), you'll feed him first.

Then what happens to him while *you* eat? Or come to that, when you're in the lounge, or at the bar? To keep him sitting still or imprisoned in your bedroom is cruel, and to allow him to crawl or march about is unfair to everybody else.

"Solutions"

One answer, of course, is to stay at a hotel that caters to babies and young children, with meals planned specifically for them, diaper service, baby-sitting arrangements, and all the rest. Apart from the fact that you'll be surrounded by other people's children—on your vacation, yet—it could cost you plenty.

So could the other solution: renting a cottage or an apartment. You're on your own, with nobody to object to your baby playing in the middle of the floor, and you have all the facilities of home. Apart from a change of scene, though, are you really having a vacation? You have all your usual chores to do, but you are hampered by an unfamiliar vacuum-cleaner and an electric stove when you're used to gas.

And for the money you'd pay out for a really good cottage or apartment or a family hotel for the three of you, you and your husband could have a package-tour of Europe, or live it up in Hawaii. You'd have to leave the baby behind, though, and as I said earlier, such a parting needs working up to gradually.

Even while staying with someone they like, few babies could accept mother's absence for more than a week in their first year, and not all could do so even in their second year. If you have real doubts about whether your child will be happy with your sister Molly for two weeks, don't go. You'd never relax for worrying. Skip the vacation, save the money, and wait till Junior will enjoy going with you.

And when is that? Not for several years, I fear. The color pictures in the brochures—mother, father and three children playing volley ball on a beach—do not apply to us. There is no vacation activity that the whole family can enjoy that would include a child under five. Virtually everything you and your husband might want to do on vacation conflicts with the needs and desires of your youngster. You want to have a quiet drink at a shady table in an open-air café; your under-five, once he's finished his orange drink or ice cream, wants to play on the beach. He is engrossed in a street puppet show but you want to drag him back to the hotel because it's drizzling. You have been invited to a cocktail party at the Palace Hotel by a wealthy couple you've just met. However, the party will be between five and seven, which is when you give your three-year-old dinner. See what I mean?

You have spent fifty weeks of this year, never stopping for a cup of coffee when you are out shopping, turning down social invitations whenever you can't find a baby-sitter, going out for walks to feed the ducks when it's cold and you'd rather be indoors; and you painted a rosy picture for yourself of these two weeks being different. You imagined that your husband and child would play together, that Daddy would enjoy building sand castles, paddling, playing with a football, and taking Junior for walks looking for pretty shells. And so he does—for half an hour at a stretch. If you nag him to do more he's likely to resent you and the child, and regret the money he has spent, and moan about having to "work" during his vacation.

I know it's unfair, because he is a parent too, but that's the way it is. To add insult to injury, fathers are wont to complain when they see their wives washing children's clothes before being able to get out for the day, and they grumble about all the paraphernalia that is vital for an hour on the beach.

Why only an hour when the sun's been shining all afternoon? Because your two-and-a-half-year-old sleeps from 2 o'clock till 3:30. I admit that most children over two can be trained out of sleep during the day, but one can't "train" him out of getting tired and irritable. Once you've kept your child from his afternoon nap for fourteen days during your vacation, you'll find he won't go back to napping once he's home again. Bang goes that welcome break for you. He'll still be tired but won't lie down.

Americans Abroad

Most of these objections are equally true of the vacation abroad, and I can add some more. The money your husband's "wasting" is an even larger amount for just the same old beach-routine. The leisurely swim with your husband in the warm Adriatic never happens because one of you has always to be in the shallows with the child. You miss most of the Uffizi Gallery in Florence because the child is bored and begins to cry. You don't see Venice because the child isn't up to the trip, and you may not be able to afford Italy again for years.

Although illness abroad is not quite so menacing as with a baby, it is still a deterrent. Two- to five-year-olds are more susceptible to infection than older children, more likely to be affected by sunstroke. If your child becomes ill while abroad, talking with a doctor in a foreign language is far from easy. Even if you speak some French or Italian or Spanish, would you understand the medical terms? And nursing a sick child in a hotel room or a villa and giving your order for a one-minute egg and a glass of peach juice in sign language to the chamber-maid could be a nightmare.

Either-Or

So what it amounts to is that you and your husband can have a vacation for yourselves or one for your child, but you

212

can't have the two in one. Let's consider *your* vacation first. While you two fly off to Majorca, or look at Viking settlements in the Hebrides, or swallow a dose of culture in Florence, it's back to loving, long-suffering Grandma for your child. If Grandmother is unable to cope, or is going off to Alaska herself, it might be possible to make a reciprocal arrangement with close friends or neighbors: you'll mind their children for two weeks in June, and they'll take your Katie in August.

Now we come to your child's vacation, which may be additional to your own or instead of it. Make up your minds beforehand that this vacation is for the child's benefit, because the older he grows beyond the age of two, the more he will appreciate a new environment. So consider his staying with friends who live in the country, where there may be animals, where there is a meadow to play in, and a shallow brook in which to paddle and float sticks. Or perhaps you can find an old-fashioned family farm or a ranch that takes summer boarders.

Again, you can rent a bungalow at the seashore or stay at a family hotel. But don't expect too much fun yourself. This kind of vacation is for your child.

29

When Mother Goes to Work

So far I have discussed baby-sitting on an irregular basis, mainly for social reasons. Now I'd like to talk about baby-sitting or child-minding as a daily routine while Mother goes out to work.

I omitted the working mother from the previous age group because, as you will have gathered, I believe a child should not be asked to accept long partings from Mother during his first year. I have kept stressing the word "gradual," for it is not gentle weaning for a child to be placed with a baby-sitter for five hours Monday to Friday.

If you have to work for pressing economic reasons— and by pressing, I mean you can't meet the food bill by

Wednesday—that's different. Like the absence of father during the day, it's sad but it has to be endured.

Resenting the Child

No, I'm speaking of the wife who yearns for the career life, or who desires the extras, like a new sofa or a real vacation that the income from a part-time job may provide. Whether or not a woman wants to work is something she has to figure out for herself, with the aid of her husband. It is, however, true that there are few things worse than a mother who feels frustrated at being cooped up at home with small children. She is so busy dreaming of greener grass that she doesn't enjoy the time she spends with her youngsters.

Consciously or subconsciously, she may very well come to blame them for her imprisonment, and that makes for an unhappy mother-and-child relationship. If she tells them of her resentment, she'll distress them; if she keeps it to herself, she'll turn into a martyr. Thus, it is better for this woman to go to work and use the money she earns to pay for child care.

I was one of these myself. With each of my three children, I recognized that as they emerged from babyhood we weren't really having fun together. I wasn't appreciating being a mother because I was constantly aware of the lack of adult company, of stimulation. So I compromised. When my first baby was about a year old, I took a part-time job.

215

I didn't get much out of it financially because most of what I earned went for my lunches, my bus fares, and what I had to pay the sitter for four hours a day. But I welcomed the break from being a housewife and, strangely enough, began to look forward to getting back home again. All in all, I enjoyed my toddler much more, and I'm sure she enjoyed me more.

I certainly do not mean that the woman who is content to be at home looking after her children, the woman who would rather suffer some economic hardship than leave them regularly in someone else's care, is not just as good a mother and person. She is. I have a daughter who is in exactly this position. She had an interesting job before she was married but now she is completely satisfied, at the age of twenty-three, to be a housewife and mother. And an excellent job she's making of her role, too.

What I'm sure *is* undesirable is being unable to come to terms with how you feel about this question of career versus motherhood. So you must discuss the problem with your husband, make a decision . . . and then accept it without miserable periods of introspection and remorse.

In this section, I'm not speaking of extremes. I'm not referring to the woman who is so possessive of her child that she cannot bear anyone taking her place, even temporarily, and who uses "maternal dedication" as an excuse for ceasing to be a wife—or indeed, a human being. Nor do I mean the woman who goes out to work leaving her children to roam about with door-keys round their necks and vague instructions to knock on Mrs. Jones' door if they want anything. I'm talking about the moderate, responsible woman who makes a compromise between home and career that suits both herself and her children.

Day Care

It's possible that you could pair off with a stay-at-home mother—i.e., while you work, you pay a friend who has chosen to stay home with her children to take care of your offspring as well (or vice-versa). But if that is not possible, then you'll have to utilize a professional who takes care of a number of children at a time in her own house. (Since she isn't a baby-sitter, let's call her a baby-minder, as the English do.)

Check out her references and assure yourself that her care is up to a certain standard. Before enrolling your child with her, talk to her when she has other children in her home, so you can see for yourself whether the place is clean and how the children react to her.

Needless to say, if your child resists the baby-minder, I'm afraid you will just have to resign from your job and, once again, work up to this sort of separation gradually, for the sake of your child's future welfare. You are not a bad mother just because you want a career—but you are if you allow your ambition to damage your child psychologically.

So if your child remains playful, responsive, and boisterous, and greets you gladly but calmly when you pick him up at the end of your workday, then all is well. But

217

beware of the converse of any of these things, or if your child undergoes changes in temperament that you cannot justify simply by the fact that he is growing up—for instance, if a normally contented, extroverted child turns into an irritable, introverted one; or if he suddenly falls victim to feeding troubles, skin disorders, and disturbed sleep; or if he returns to pants-wetting. These physical irregularities could have emotional roots. He may be suffering from loneliness or fear that you've rejected him.

It is only fair to point out that if you ignore these symptoms of your toddler's insecurity, the trouble may not show immediately but manifest itself later, when the cause is no longer obvious. I much prefer showing you how to prevent problems to having to tell you what to do about them after they have arisen.

All this being so, I do not wish to alarm you into quitting your job at the first hint of a missed meal or a cranky mood. Give yourself a fair chance. Before deciding that your child cannot cope with the new arrangements, make certain that his irritability isn't just a crotchety week (even the best of us have them), or the skin disorder merely a heat rash.

Nursery School

When your child is between three and five he can attend a nursery school, and you may be tempted to take on a larger part-time or even a full-time job. I would warn you, though, that you may find a job combined with your cleaning and shopping and washing, plus the physical care of an active youngster, too exhausting. When you collect your child each afternoon, all you may be able to do in terms of energy is give him a hurried supper and dump him in bed.

This won't do. The child wouldn't have a mother to cuddle, play with, and talk to. He'd see her only at breakfast as she dashed about organizing her day, and then again for half an hour in the evening. Certainly he would see you during weekends, but I've known far too many working mothers who were so tired by Saturday that all they wanted to do was sink into an armchair.

If you haven't the stamina for both career and motherhood, I strongly recommend you settle for the latter. (It's a little late for you now to do otherwise.) You will have plenty of opportunity later, when your child is older and away six hours daily at school, for pursuing a career. But you have only the present for shaping your child's emotional background.

Even if you *can* cope with, say, a six-hour working day, it is still possible your child won't. He may find a full morning at nursery school followed by an afternoon with the sitter too long a separation from you. He may tell you so. But if he doesn't, how will you know?

Well, if he has been the bouncy, mischievous piece of humanity we all know as a happy child, one who feels secure in the love of his parents, and he suddenly becomes quiet and hardly seems to take an interest in what's going on around him—beware. Most particularly, take warning if the sitter reports how *good* he is, meaning he sits obediently in a chair all afternoon. Normal children are not like that. So the child who is sitting quietly is actually withdrawing into himself, probably because he is deeply disturbed.

Equally, if your child plays all day, laughs, eats, but as soon as you appear he becomes angry, fretful, even violent—again, look out. Don't assume he loves nursery school so much that he doesn't want to leave it. If that were so, he'd complain but still be glad to see you. No, in fact he is punishing you for having left him . . . *deserted* him.

I can only say in general terms: observe your child, and listen to the experienced advice of his nursery-school teacher. If you and she are confident that he is happy, then nothing could be better for him than the child-oriented environment of nursery school. It stimulates him; it gives him friends; it prepares him for going to school. Whether or not he is placed in the care of a sitter, too, will, of course, depend on the decision you reached.

The Housekeeper

There are among my readers women who—because their jobs are so important to them, or because they feel so unfitted for the role of housewife and mother—would prefer to use their earnings to pay someone to take over their domestic role.

It sometimes works very well, too. The housekeeper who takes a job in a home with children is usually a woman who loves them. In practical terms, also, she has much more knowhow than the average mother, who learns by trial and error on the poor eldest children. The housekeeper has learned all about changing diapers and table manners before she comes.

Incidentally, this very fact has its disadvantages. She has her own way of doing things, often rather strict ways, and you will have to accept them. There has to be an understanding: she is to be in sole charge from Monday to Friday (perhaps with Mother returning home from her job in time to kiss the children goodnight), and the parents will take over on the weekend.

I've noticed that very often these parents try to compensate for their lengthy absence by being extra-special "fun" parents when they are there. Saturdays and Sundays are absolutely packed with treats—parties, visits to the zoo, outings to the lake, family games, all accompanied by the sort of luxury presents ordinary children receive only once or twice a year. I'm not quarreling with these parents' contention that such an arrangement thrills the children and allows the parents to give them unstinting attention for two whole days. Unfortunately, the parents thus demote themselves to the roles of favorite aunt and uncle.

The sort of attachment most children form for Mother has had to be given to her substitute. Because the housekeeper is the one who's always there, she's the person the child automatically goes to for his daily needs—because he is hurt, because he's unhappy, because he is hungry. So if you're contemplating the use of a professional housekeeper, face up to the penalty now. You mustn't feel jealous or wounded if, when your child cries, he cries for your housekeeper rather than you.

To sum up: I firmly believe the ideal is still a home with a loving amateur mother and father in it and not a substitute-dominated nursery, however well-run it might be.

30

Being Afraid

We'd all be afraid, I suppose, if we were confronted by a pack of wolves in the middle of a forest. That sort of fear is logical, and sometimes even essential to our survival. But constant fear of encountering a wolf when one lives in the heart of a city, that's *illogical*. That sort of fear is a phobia. Young children in particular suffer from phobias.

The first thing to say about phobias is that, although they are nonsense to other people, they are only too real to their victims. The main thing to remember in every attack of phobia is that the immediate circumstance is the trigger, and the phobia itself, whatever it may be, is based on the fear of an unknown.

223

If you fear spiders or snakes or waterfalls, you know what I'm talking about. You will understand that it only makes the fear worse if you are told, "Now, don't be stupid, just fight it out." Equally, if you're overprotected from meeting the experience you dread, you'll never have a chance to get used to it and conquer it.

I myself am terrified of thunderstorms. Now, if someone had stood me out in the middle of a field or even forced me to stand by a window during a thunderstorm, I would prabably be even more frightened of them than I am.

No one did. Instead, my mother went to the other extreme, for she, too, was terrified of thunderstorms. Whenever one started she would crawl under the dining-room table with a blanket over her head and me clasped to her bosom. No wonder I still have this phobia.

I did have enough restraint, though, not to repeat my mother's behavior with my own children, and they are not nervous about thunderstorms. They know not to stand under a solitary tree, but they have no illogical fear of thunder and lightning. In fact, while I huddle with the cat and the dog, they happily count the seconds between flash and roar and calculate the distance of the bolt. (Incidentally, in the course of controlling myself while my children were small and impressionable, I have overcome a good deal of my own fear.)

Mothers Are Human, Too

It's important, I think, to say here that you're not a failure as a parent just because your child knows you have a phobia. It's bad only if you infect him with it. It may even be a good thing for him to learn while still young that you're only human, and that he must be considerate of your fears just as you're considerate of his. This is up to Father. He must explain that Mother is afraid of mice, let us say, and that we therefore never tease her with them.

I never minded that the children knew I was frightened of house mice. But I couldn't rationalize for them *why* I was frightened. I still can't. I have handled white laboratory mice without repulsion. I stroke bigger "mice," like guinea pigs. But show me a wee brown mouse nibbling in the pantry and I can barely suppress a scream. I've found that observing one from a safe distance, knowing I can always retreat, and then approaching a bit closer the next day does help me come to terms with my phobia.

And this, I firmly believe, is the method one should adopt in teaching one's children to overcome their strange fears. Always use a gradual approach. The child may fear the parakeet or a new house or a hanging lamp with a fringed crimson shade. Let him examine it at a distance before going closer, and the moment you see signs of panic, stop, retreat a step, comfort and reassure. Next day try again.

It is generally true to say that if you yourself are of an anxious temperament, if you tend to worry about things that your friends take in stride, this anxiety pervades the atmosphere and will tend to produce an anxious child. Well, at least you'll sympathize with his fears, which to some extent compensates him for not being the robust, daring little fellow your friends have.

Sometimes, of course, the Fates issue to happy-go-lucky parents who welcome challenges a child who is the exact opposite. If you are in this situation, I beg you to show extra understanding to your sensitive, withdrawn little one. He has his contribution to make as a human being, but if you try to force him to make it your way, bravely and heartily, you could easily break him completely.

Some Common Phobias

So let's talk in detail about some of the more common phobias of early childhood and how to deal with them. Obviously there will be many, many others which I haven't room to deal with in this book. On those I'd give the same advice: watch your child and use the gradual approach.

A baby under three months may be frightened of a mobile over his crib, or of the wallpaper in his room. If he screams, pick him up soothingly and carry him away from whatever upset him. But the best way to combat this sort of phobia is to avoid it. Make sure the room you choose for your nursery does not have a loud paper that might scare him. Remember that if he's born in the hospital, he may well spend the first ten days of his life looking at plain

226

cream walls. Quite a shock, therefore, coming home to scarlet and purple whirls! Likewise, if a super-sophisticated young aunt buys him a grotesque stuffed animal, put it away in a cupboard until he is old enough to think it funny.

Another phobia of young babies is of sudden loud noises, such as the banging of a door or the very shrill ring of a telephone. Obviously you cannot live in a tomb; if your door bangs and other members of the family forget that it does, then baby is going to be exposed to his phobia over and over again. You can try posting a notice on the door saying: "Please Close Gently," but the best thing to do is to move Baby's crib as far away from the front door or the phone as possible.

And when he does cry in terror, comfort him *calmly*. Gradually he'll get the message that there's nothing to be frightened of. In any event, as a child grows older his nervous system becomes more accustomed to noise, even sudden noise, and he will outgrow his phobia.

Unfortunately, while he outgrows some fears, he acquires others. Between three and nine months, he may become frightened of new people, or young men, or men in uniform, different-colored people, or white-haired people, or people who wear glasses—especially dark glasses or glasses with heavy frames.

Now if, for instance, when Grandma wears her heavy-framed glasses, the child stiffens and screams with fear, there is no point in Grandma continuing to hold him clasped tightly to her breast. That's like the lion holding you in his teeth to reassure you he's not going to bite you. You have that nagging doubt that at any moment he could change his mind! You'd rather he put you down and then told you. Same with Grandma. Take the child from Grandma, and ask Grandma to take off the glasses. Then the child can observe her from a distance, and approach when he feels ready.

Many a baby under the age of a year is frightened if a human face comes too close; it's enormous to him. Yes, even if the face is making cooing noises and smiling. That's why we, as parents, have to to try to keep our loving friends and relatives at a slight distance from the baby, particularly if he has just awakened, particularly if he doesn't know them, and particularly if they're wearing something which he might take exception to, such as a large hat.

It's possible, too, that he can suddenly be scared stiff of you. A young mother told me that one day she picked up her baby and he stiffened (that's usually a symptom of this sort of fear), screamed, and tried to get away from her. "It's Mother," she kept saying, cuddling him, and the more she cuddled him, the more frantic he became.

Eventually she gave up trying to soothe him and put him in his high-chair for his supper, thus unconsciously removing him a few inches from his bugbear. He was then sufficiently reassured by her familiar voice and the routine of eating to stop crying, but he kept a wary eye on something just above her head. She examined the wall behind her, and the ceiling, then suddenly realized what it was that frightened him. She was wearing hair rollers, and he had never seen her with them before.

She did the sensible thing in the circumstances. She took out one of the yellow plastic rollers to prove that it was harmless, played with it, and showed him it was light and could roll about. Finally he dared to hold it. But he took all that convincing to realize that Mommy was really Mommy, and that, even if she was, she didn't have a monster side to her.

Another little thing that often frightens a baby is if a piece of furniture is not in its accustomed place, or if his crib has been moved so that he sees the room from an unexpected angle. If your baby suddenly goes rigid and screams for no apparent reason, look around. What have you done? What have you moved? What has changed? What is there that wasn't there before?

The play of light and shadow on a chest of drawers near a window can look like a black menace. A coat on the side of an armchair can look like a grotesque and dangerous person. *You* know what a garden umbrella is; you probably bought it so he could lie outside in his carriage and not get sunburned. But to him, unless he is carefully introduced to it, it can seem a threat. If he resists, don't leave him to its mercy, strapped down with this mushroom looming above him. Let him examine it with you, and every time he refuses to look at it, take him away and let him look at it from a distance.

It may take a few days, and you may fail even then. You may have to get rid of the umbrella. You may have to move the chest of drawers. You may have to stop the family from slinging their coats around. But it's worth giving in to keep your baby happy. Never dismiss his phobia as silly, and say he will just have to get over it. That's downright cruel, and it probably won't work anyway.

Infant Conservatism

Just now I mentioned that a baby likes his crib where he expects his crib to be. You'll sympathize if you've ever awakened to find yourself facing a wall when your bed at home is beside a low window. For a second there's a bewildered "Where am I?" until you remember you're staying with friends. But suppose you weren't an adult who could work that out . . . Then the panic would linger, wouldn't it? Solution: Don't move the nursery furniture about "for a change" the way you do the living-room furniture.

It's not only the view either. The baby likes the familiarity of the crib itself. (Babies are unashamedly conservative about most things.) So when the time comes to transfer him into a bed of his own, set the crib in the bed for a week; that way he'll grow used to his new environment.

The same applies to the promotion to the big bath. To start with, make the change by putting his baby bath in the big one. Or you can utilize the sink as an intermediary stage—from baby bath to kitchen sink to big bath.

Fear of the Sea

Now, just as babies are initially afraid of being bathed in a big tub, they also often distrust their first glimpse of the seashore. A baby who is perfectly happy crawling all over the kitchen floor, the living-room carpet, and the lawn, may sit petrified on a beautiful sandy beach. Well, think of the noise of the sea, and this vast expanse of dun-colored floor that is so different from the linoleum and wool and grass he's used to.

So, before he starts wailing inconsolably, I recommend that you spread down a blanket—a small blanket that he knows, perhaps his own baby blanket—and indicate to him that this is his territory. He will feel safe on the blanket and he can explore beyond its frontiers in his own time.

Some toddlers, too, are none too happy beside the sea. Again, it's too vast for them. I'm sure you've seen an eighteen-month-old standing alone in the sand, his mouth puckered, his eyes searching desperately for a face he knows. So, to start with, he also may need to remain within the confines of your "camp"—your circle of beach chairs, buckets, clothes, and towels—and venture out only when he can hold your hand.

I have already touched upon the under-fives' common phobia about moving water, when we discussed swimming. I would add to this that if you don't live on or near the coast, the mere sight of swirling sea would be a totally new experience for your child. So take it gently. Introduce him first to the paddling pool in the park, and work up to the children's end of the swimming pool, and eventually progress to an excursion to the seashore, or a lake or river. At any sign of fear—crying, clutching you or, more seriously, going stiff and silent—come out of the water and try again a few days later.

231

Fear of the Dark

I also mentioned in passing, this time in connection with discipline, the child who becomes afraid of the dark. Just because your toddler used to sleep perfectly happily without a light on doesn't mean he's kidding you now. As his environment and knowledge increase, so regrettably do the number of things he's afraid of. The old argument that everybody sleeps in the dark one day and so the child had better stop this nonsense now—and with this the parent closes the door on him—is unkind and unnecessary. You won't cure him like that, and in fact you don't need to cure him at all. He will cure himself, provided he isn't abandoned to his fear at this tender age.

A soft night-light that gives a glow to his room but is not bright enough to be disturbing, or simply a landing or hall light left on, is usually enough. It may even be sufficient to have the bedroom door ajar so that he has the background comfort of hearing voices, water running, the television. It will let him know there are people out there—people who will protect him from this black abyss.

Agoraphobes and Claustrophobes

Between two and five years of age, many children feel comfortable only in a small enclosed space. For some, it can be an obsession. A friend of mine who runs a nursery told me that she once had a little girl who was a chronic agoraphobe—a hater of open space. The nursery had a number of wooden boxes that were used for games and as tables at milk time. Well, this little girl would retreat into one of the boxes and sit there, cramped and in the dark, for long periods. Then she would suddenly come out, play happily a while and climb back into her box.

Now, it would have been very tempting to insist that, since she enjoyed being with the other children, she stay out and involve herself in the group activity. But my friend understood that the little girl herself would decide when she no longer required what Freud would call "the womb symbol." She very wisely left her to it, and I'm glad to report that over the months the child needed her box less and less. She now seems to be very well integrated into the class; she's laughing and splashing and is just as active and makes just as much noise as the other children.

So, if your child develops a habit of playing in a dim corner, don't fish him out; don't even coax him out. Just be welcoming when he emerges, and keep a casual eye on him over the next year to make sure he is returning to his corner less and less frequently rather than more and more. If the latter is true, then there is something radically wrong in his world, and you both need expert help.

I don't want to seem depressing, but for every infant agoraphobe, there are probably two claustrophobes—children who fear confined spaces. Perhaps an older child has gone to the closet under the stairs to get out the vacuum cleaner and the little one has trotted after her. And the older child, in fun, has pretended to lock the baby in the closet. The very suggestion can be enough to set off a horrible train of thought in the child's mind.

Worse, some women even use "locking him up" as a method of controlling a child. "If you don't behave, I'll put you in the broom closet . . ." Do you wonder, incidentally, that I said choose your sitter with care?

It's hard to cure a child of claustrophobia. Many adults are grappling with the problem without success. That's why I'm so insistent on preventing it in the first place. However, if your child, through no fault of yours, does develop this phobia, I can only suggest the obvious: Promise him faithfully that you will never leave him in the closet under the stairs, if that's what's worrying him. Show him conversationally that there's a light there anyway. And bear with him about taking the escalator in stores and not exploring caves on vacation. With calmness and forethought on your part and a growing trust on his, he may have a fighting chance of overcoming his morbid fear.

Let's turn to a less drastic fear. Almost all children of this age hate having their hair washed. I know I used to bellow like a small bull, I was so scared of getting my face wet. Non-sting shampoo has subdued many of the loudest complaints, but there still remains the business of water gushing over one's face and threatening to drown one.

After battling with each of my own three children, I found a way around it. I placed a kitchen chair in front of the wash basin in the bathroom and stood with one foot firmly on the chair and the child lying backwards across my thigh with his head in the basin. It's a crude imitation of the way the girl shampoos you at the hairdresser's. But it works, because the child's face is no longer close to the water, and so it's much less frightening. Admittedly you can only use one hand for washing (the other arm grasping the child round the chest to stop him slipping off), but I reckon that's easier, and certainly more pleasant, than struggling with a yelling victim.

Nightmares

For a child, nightmares are even worse than shampoos. A youngster of two or two-and-a-half may well wake screaming from a bad dream and fail to appreciate that the experience was not reality. The trouble is at that age he's unlikely to articulate clearly: He won't be able to tell you something buzzed at him and hurt him and he couldn't get away. He'll more probably just sob and, at best, mutter: "Bee . . . bee . . ." It's up to you to catch on.

Comfort him until he's soothed but, equally important, explain about dreams in principle. Tell him that while he's in bed pictures are produced in his head and it's like watching television while he's asleep. He may see himself and Mommy in the park or the animals from his picture book playing together; but he only pictures these things. And the funny thing about dreams is that the pictures are all jumbled up together. (By then he will understand about jumbled pictures because he will have played card games and mixed up the cards.)

He'll also be relieved to know that everybody—not just

he—sees pictures when they're asleep, and that some of the pictures are nice and some of them not so nice.

As far as I know, dreams are likely to be imponderables only with a first child, because second and subsequent children hear older brothers and sisters talk about them. I know from my own children that my youngest looked forward to having a dream because it was a sort of sign of being older.

Food Phobias

A totally different sort of phobia children have is over certain foods. They object violently to something you serve; it has nothing to do with the flavor; it's the texture. For them, it conjures up disgusting associations. Spinach feels like slime, macaroni like worms. When this happens, I advise you to take away quietly whatever bothers him and exclude it from his diet in the future.

Curiously enough, the association may be subconscious; he may not have the vocabulary to express why he hates his hard-boiled egg so much. You will recognize it's a texture phobia only from the magnitude of the reaction, which is a far cry from "I don't like potatoes; they're dumb." And unlike the potatoes that come around at the next meal regardless, hard-boiled eggs never darken his plate again. That doesn't mean the rest of the family can't eat them. They should, because, apart from the fact they've a right to, it gives the child an opportunity to say one day:

236

"Well, I suppose I could have a little egg—not much, just a little . . ." And, of course, this is the child's instinctive way of using the gradual approach to master his phobia.

In conclusion I would repeat something I said at the outset, that *your* anxiety fans his. This applies to physical as well as psychological upsets. There's a golden rule to apply when your child bangs his head or scrapes a knee. Wait! Wait for the child's own reaction to his injury. If he dusts himself off, picks himself up and carries on, swallow your concern and do something else. If he cries because he really has hurt himself, give sympathetic but firm and friendly help, and administer whatever first aid—a kiss or something more practical—is necessary.

I've discovered Band-Aids are not only a protection for a graze, but almost a badge of battle. I've used many Band-Aids in places that weren't injured enough to need them. It works like the teething jellies I mentioned, and it's worth the waste of Band-Aids.

Now, suppose you've been reading this chapter very carefully and you have grown more and more discouraged as you have gone along. You have a child who is a coward about his wounds; he's frightened of the dark; he's scared of strangers; he's terrified of water and confined spaces and, in addition, he has a few phobias of his very own that I haven't mentioned at all. Your husband considers the child weak and accuses you of spoiling or pampering and, if it's a boy, perhaps he even despises him as a "sissy." What do you do to toughen him up, to breach this gulf between your menfolk?

You accept. You accept you have a highly sensitive

child who needs extra loving, not doubting. For whatever your husband may or may not say in the child's presence, your child will be well aware of his attitude. And to feel a failure to the parents he loves on top of being frightened of almost every new experience must be unbearable. It would drive him further into himself—instead of out. He'd never become that brave little man your husband, and perhaps you, were hoping for. So you love him as he is, and you use the gradual reach-withdraw mechanism to cope with his many fears. And who knows—with the spur of your own and your husband's approval, he may even win a few of his own wars.

31

Those "Bad" Habits

Many parents worry that their children have developed "bad" habits, such as thumb-sucking, and wonder what to do about them. Let's see, beginning with the thumb-sucking.

Sucking is instinctive. Some babies suck thumbs or forefingers while still in the womb. It seems to be a way of achieving relaxation and contentment. And no adult can say with certainty how much sucking time—as distinct from milk-taking time—any one baby needs.

You will notice that children, and indeed many adults, sleep in a position very similar to the one they had in the womb. In sleep, they return to the safe world in which they spent so many months of development. But your baby can't reach this haven unless he has as many factors as possible representing the womb-like state: darkness, firm wrapping, being well-fed, content, and lying in the same position, curled and sucking a finger.

The trouble with sucking thumbs or fingers outside the womb is that it can result in mouth and stomach infections, lead to misshapen fingers, and malform the gums. So for the baby under six months who has an extra need to suck, fingers and thumbs are undesirable. But more undesirable still is to deprive him of what he needs.

The Security Prop

The solution is the much-maligned pacifier. The baby who has enough security, love, and food, and is not sick or in pain will tend to want a pacifier only when he is tired or just before falling asleep. Don't worry that he'll always want one—that would be as abhorrent to me as it is to you. If your baby needs a pacifier, keep two, so that when one is in use, there's always another sterilized and ready.

As your baby gets to be older than six months, he may prefer a companion to a pacifier. This could be something like a muslin diaper or a stuffed rabbit. He hasn't got the makings of a neurotic because he refuses to settle down to sleep without it. He'll grow up perfectly normal provided you indulge him in this—even to taking his "security blanket" or whatever it is along when he spends a night away from home. Don't ever try to substitute a socially

240

more acceptable toy for whatever he cherishes. He will make the replacement himself when he is ready, and this may not be until he is four.

But if he insists on the company of his "security blanket" when he's up and about, that's different. I happen to know a two-year-old who drags his muslin diaper along where other children would take their Teddy bears. This little boy is perfectly well-adjusted; he simply regards "Bibby" as a friend.

And who are we to say that a square of material hasn't got a face, a body, and two arms, and therefore cannot possibly be a companion? Even so, apart from the matter of hygiene—dragging "Bibby" through the mud and then nuzzling it is far from sanitary—such dependence on any one thing is to be discouraged. Just as we, as mothers, have weaned our toddler away from our constant companionship by occasionally leaving him with a sitter, so he should be weaned away from his stuffed rabbit or muslin diaper. Try leaving it in his bed (ready for sleep-time) when he comes into the living room to play. You may be surprised to find that he'll be so engrossed with his pull-along truck, he won't even miss it. If he does, and shows signs of stress, let him have it back. He obviously needs some sort of security prop.

That, in one sentence, is why a continual need for a "companion" is serious: it means there's something in his life that makes him insecure. Find out what that is, and put it right; the "security blanket" will be dispensed with after a time.

In the same way, thumb-sucking during the day may be a security prop—or it may just be something to do because a

241

child is bored. One never sees a child who is happily occupied sucking his thumb. So if you have a thumb-sucker, ask yourself: are the toys he's been offered the wrong sort to stimulate him? (This is particularly true of a story you may be telling him: it's too difficult, or too boringly easy, and so he reckons he'll suck his thumb instead of paying attention.) Have you inadvertently made him too passive, insisting that he sit quietly with a picture book or a box of dominoes for a large part of his day?

Of course, never smack a child for sucking his thumb. This would only lead him to do it secretly, and that would make the habit more obsessive than ever.

With the child who sits thumb-sucking in a corner of his crib instead of sleeping, I suspect the answer is plain: he's fed up to the back teeth—if you'll pardon the expression—with his crib. He's obviously having more rest than he needs, and instead of screaming his complaint at you, he's gone apathetic. So beware. If your child continually (say, for over a week) doesn't sleep for one particular rest period, he's cut that one out.

Now, if you're wailing that your child no longer has any naps during the day but is still not tired when he goes to bed at eight—he sits there sucking his thumb, staring vacantly into space—then you've a rare one indeed. I suspect his bed is too sterile—by that I mean no cuddly animals (companions) in it, no pictures on the wall for him to look at. I am not recommending he be given toys at night-time—construction kits and toy trucks. But the odd friend to talk to drowsily, that's different.

Masturbation

More worrisome than thumb-sucking to many parents is masturbation. A lot of babies (especially boys) discover that fingering their genitals brings a pleasant sensation, and as they get to be two or three years old they tend to do it to comfort themselves when they're tired or ill. I'm relieved that the Victorian reaction to masturbation—an unpardonable sin, "cured" by whippings, by warnings that it would drive one mad, or by tying the child's hands to the bedstead—has passed. Today, most mothers realize that any sort of punishment could make a child ashamed of his sexual organs, which could in turn one day distort his attitude toward sex.

However, this doesn't stop a mother from being embarrassed by the sight of her one-year-old handling his penis in the bath. I've heard other child experts say that, if you are in this category, it is perfectly all right to divert your infant's attention—pass him his boat to play with, for instance. I quarrel with this advice. If on every occasion when your child begins to masturbate, you immediately urge him, however subtly, to stop, he'll very soon know that this is something of which Mommy disapproves. So personally, I would say to embarrassed mothers: find something to divert your own attention. Polish the taps of the basin or something, until he's finished.

By the time your child has outgrown babyhood, masturbation will instinctively have become a private thing, confined to his bed. And should your four- or five-year-old start doing it in the living room, take him to his bed without any comment or indication of censure. In this way, he'll absorb the idea that while masturbation isn't terrible or wrong, it is not socially acceptable in public.

Finally, if the habit seems to you to be practiced excessively, you should consult your pediatrician. The child may be emotionally disturbed.

Nose-Picking

A really horrible habit is nose-picking. I have a theory that it starts after a cold (and one- to five-year-olds have an awful lot of colds) when the mucus dries up in little lumps in the nostrils. The child removes them with his finger and finds this stops the irritation. And from that moment, his mother will be saying: "Not your finger, dear; use a tissue . . ."

So to follow through logically: if whenever you wash your child's face, you check that his nose is clean, too, the desire to nose-pick should never arise.

For babies and toddlers, absorbent cotton Q-tips are ideal for nose-care. (Or so my daughter tells me—actually, I get on better with a tissue.) For later on, I suggest you have a box of clean tissues in every key room in the house, because "up in the front bedroom" can seem a long way to a child with a picking-finger poised. Nose hygiene should also prevent that other ghastly habit: sniffling.

Nail-Biting

As for nail-biting, I ought to confess right away that I was a nail-biter myself. My mother tried everything under the sun to stop me, and nothing worked. But where a mother may fail over some thirteen years, a first love succeeds quickly. There I was, in romantic pre-war Vienna, fifteen years old and wildly in love with a blond and handsome Austrian. I shall never forget it: he lifted my hand to his lips to kiss, he held my bitten-away fingernails—and he quietly put my hand down again, without the kiss. I never bit my nails again.

Still, for parents who are not prepared to wait thirteen years for a cure, the best idea is to say nothing when you notice your small child nibbling at his fingernails, but at wash-time paint on Thumb or Bitex, products your druggist should have. Tell your child chattily that it's to make his nails look pretty, and put some on your own to prove the point. Then pray. If you're lucky, the next time he puts his fingers into his mouth, the nasty taste of quinine will put him off nail-biting for life. He must never, however, suspect that you engineered the whole thing.

Be prepared for failure, though. Determined nail-biters can even acquire a taste for quinine. I know, because my younger daughter did. I've used every argument on Merle my mother used on me, and none of them stopped her. What eventually did the trick—you've guessed it—was a boyfriend.

There are hundreds of annoying little habits that

children can adopt—from twitching an ear to wiggling a piece of string. I think it's all right to mention it once, or even twice. "Look, do you suppose your ear enjoys being pulled like that? If I were your ear, I wouldn't . . ." Sometimes, just being aware one has a certain gesture is sufficient to enable one to control it.

But treat it lightly. And if at all possible, unobtrusively find something more constructive to do for the offending hand or whatever. Never nag about it or continually draw attention to it; that only makes it worse. It's like the smoker who needs a cigarette to fiddle with. Should you ask him why he wants something in his hand, he'll become more aware of his idle fingers, not less.

You may regard some habit your child has as really anti-social and deserving of smacks. Well, that's your decision as a parent. But I have a hunch punishment won't help. I believe there are some people who need seemingly useless physical activity to offset the mental activity of concentration—whether it's the four-year-old playing dolls or an adult like Patricia, who during her grueling editing of this book chewed up five whole pencils!

32

Your Child and Other Animals

You may recognize that this title is cribbed from Gerald Durrell, a man I admire very much. It refers to your child in relationship to your friends, your child in relationship to his own friends, and your child in relationship to animals—the four-legged kind, both your own and other people's.

Let me say right away that there is no reason why your friends, even your closest friends, should be as enamored of your child as you are, and vice versa. I had a friend who was like a sister to me, but my elder daughter, then about six months old, screamed whenever she came near. Since Tina had seen the friend frequently before and nothing about the friend's appearance or manner had changed, we concluded that my baby simply didn't like my friend.

After that, my friend, a sensible woman, kept her distance—instead of cuddling Tina, she ignored her. And there was no more trouble. No one was upset. I wasn't, my friend wasn't, and Tina was downright relieved. So if a baby can take exception to a particular person for some reason all her own, how much more intensely can a four-year-old have a special—and to you, unfounded—dislike?

Civility If Not Love

That's fair enough. But it doesn't mean your child should be permitted to behave rudely. He may come out anyway with such bald statements as "I don't like you"; if he does, he should be reprimanded, because hurting visitors' feelings is unkind and inhospitable.

Parents should insist that their children be as polite and as well behaved toward their friends as their age allows. They should say "hello," "good-bye," "please," "thank you," and all the normal things that oil the wheels of social relationships. Good gracious, your child is probably going to dislike somebody one day much more than he does your friend Marjorie. And that somebody is likely to be a person he's *got* to be polite to—his history teacher, his boss, his sister-in-law. So he might as well get used to the conventions now. We can demand polite behavior but we cannot (and shouldn't attempt to) enforce a loving relationship where no love exists.

You will also have friends who, charming though they

may be, just don't like young children, or—dreadful thought—just don't like your particular child. I occasionally find that people whom I personally like very much have children whom I have very little time for—children not reared with common sense. Yet I still like the parents. Come to that, over the years we have made many friends who hadn't the slightest interest in *our* children.

The point is this: if friends seem uncomfortable in your child's presence, my advice is not to try to seduce them by putting your little girl in a pretty, frilly dress and lecturing her on manners, but just to accept that we all have our preferences. While I don't think you ought to banish your daughter from the living room when such friends arrive, you certainly can avoid shoving her down their throats. Don't let her pester them to play with her (that goes for the most sentimental child-lover too: only the guest who really wants to should have to read a story), and watch what you do with her in front of them. Don't change her diaper in the room where they're sitting. Don't eat the soggy remnants of her lunch. That kind of thing can put your friends off you, and children in general, for ever.

By the way, I think it unnecessary for every acquaintance to be called "Aunt" or "Uncle." If you are on first-name terms with somebody, surely now, in the twentieth century, it should be perfectly polite for your children also to address them as "Jean" or "Peter." If Jean and Peter object, that's different.

Children under five often cannot understand who is and who is not a member of the family. I have seen considerable confusion arise over who is a proper aunt, or a proper uncle, and who is an "improper uncle." Reserve "Aunt" and "Uncle" for relatives.

Incidentally, when you are visiting Jean and Peter in the evening, I recommend putting your child to bed in their house at his usual bedtime with his usual ritual: bath, pajamas, Teddy, and all. Then at 11 or 12 P.M., all you need do is carry the sleepy child in a thick blanket out to the car and into his bed once you're home. It avoids both curtailing your evening and getting your child overtired.

Coping with Adult Conversation

One final appeal before we leave the subject of your friends; never, never discuss your child with them in the child's hearing. Praise will make him vain; criticism will make him feel inferior and betrayed; and simply talking about him will make him self-conscious. General conversation which includes the child ("We went to the zoo yesterday, and Johnnie had a ride on the elephant—didn't you Johnnie . . .") is different and beneficial. But discussing him ('Johnnie started nursery school last week and he seemed shy of the other children . . .') is unforgivable.

I often meet in the street mothers whose children I helped deliver. "Look, Matthew," they say, "this is the lady who brought you into the world." I can see poor Matthew squirm with embarrassment. Then, blessedly, Mother passes on to the weather, her vacation, Grandpa's arthritis, and all the ordinary grown-ups' chatter and Matthew, though bored stiff, can at least relax.

I would add that children find adult conversation awfully dull. As a five-year-old myself I suffered interminable afternoon teas at which I had to be seen but was never allowed to be heard. I used to go home bursting to say something. So on behalf of the current generation of young children, may I request that when they say, "Mommy . . ." and you say, "Just a moment, dear; Jean's speaking," you do remember them in a moment. When Jean has finished her sentence, you should turn to your small son or daughter and ask pleasantly and attentively what it is he or she wants to say.

Making Friends

Just as your child and your friends may not be chummy, there is no reason to suppose that your child and your friends' children will be pals. I know of many instances where the children loathe the sight of each other but are forced to spend many boring Sundays in each other's company because the parents want to spend the day together. As a result, the children become cranky and insufferable. It would be preferable to cut such daytime visits to a minimum and see the parents when their children aren't around.

The trouble is: many parents are unaware that two

three-year-olds do not necessarily make two close friends, any more than two brothers make two intimates. Put any child into a nursery school and he'll become best friends not with the whole class but with somebody or with a couple of somebodies.

Teacher will insist on politeness toward everybody in the class, like them or not, but no teacher would dream of insisting on close friendship between two children. Teachers know that friendship develops only if the two children want it to. So take a leaf out of Teacher's book: politeness to everybody, but friendship only where your child chooses.

Making Enemies

And once your child has made a choice, almost inevitably you get a "She's my best friend and I hate her" situation. Your three- to five-year-old child will begin to have squabbles and rows and scenes, not with you but with his or her own friends. Your child comes to you and complains that Billy hit him or Jane took his favorite ball or car. What do you do? Play it by ear.

I think it unwise to get involved in every squabble your child has, because it is only too easy to wind up an enemy of the parents of every child with whom he has ever played. Children fight about something and then hate each other. It doesn't last long—the next day, sometimes the next minute, they're best friends again. Not so the adults who champion them. Criticize someone's darling and a grudge may be borne against you for life. So wherever possible let your child fight his own battles and settle his own scores.

Occasionally, of course, you have to get involved. If there is physical injury (and that means injury inflicted by either side—your child is no more an angel than any other child), if he's been bashed by somebody and somebody else has a black eye, this ought to be acknowledged and amends made. A lecture, an apology, even a punishment: take whatever steps are required.

If you need to claim back a toy, an expensive toy perhaps, which you feel your child ought to keep, visit the other child's parents on a basis of "What can we adults do together about this disagreement between our children?" Do not come to them in an accusatory manner: "Your child has taken Tracy's doll's carriage. What are you going to do about it?" The desire to defend one's young is strong in all of us, so be on your guard not to provoke it in your neighbor. You shouldn't become isolated in a community just because your child is still learning about the give-and-take of human relationships.

How can you assist your child in learning this? Only, I fear, by example. The rest he'll have to find out the hard way: for himself. I mean, if a four-year-old's so bossy that other children refuse to play with him, it is to be hoped that the ensuing loneliness will make him realize the error of his ways and that the next week he will be a little more amenable when he joins in the game. The same goes for the spiteful child, or the one who won't share his toys.

If you notice an anti-social trait in your child, of course you can try pointing it out to him. But a philosophy of do-as-you-would-be-done-by ("How would you like it if Adam never let you have a turn on the tricycle?") is pretty sophisticated for an under-five to follow. He can't imagine himself in Adam's shoes, standing on the grass, and Adam becoming him racing away on the tricycle.

Example is what counts in the long run. The child will be considerate to other children if his parents are considerate to him. It isn't any good trying to stop your child from hitting and shouting if you yourself are given to sudden outbursts, during which you whack and bellow, rattling the doors and windows. Your child will also lose his temper and bellow, because this is obviously the standard you expect in your house—whatever you may say to the contrary.

Friendships for your child are absolutely essential. However, he's bound to make some friends with whom, for various reasons, you'd prefer him not to associate. Keep your cool. Don't break up the acquaintance. The more you forbid the association, the more resistance you will create in your child. (I've often thought that if the Montagues and Capulets hadn't opposed the match so violently, Romeo and Juliet might well have become bored and drifted apart.) In any case, it isn't necessary to part your child from some young friend he values. Provided your child's home is a happy one and its standards consistently high, your influence will prevail over anyone else's, especially another three- or four-year-old's.

Getting a Pet

There is a theory that it is good for children to have pets to look after. It's true, but it doesn't apply to under-five-year-olds. Certainly it is good for them to live with animals in the house, but don't imagine that your child will look after the puppy you give him for Christmas. (Personally, I object to an animal belonging to a particular member of the family anyway—since it lives with the family, it will be fed, bathed, walked, and played with by everyone.)

A child under five cannot undertake such responsibility. You still have to buy the food, you still have to see that the dog's bedding is changed. The child cannot groom the dog, although he can help, and he can't go off and walk the dog for an hour—not under the age of five. If the pet's been involved in a fight, you have to deal with the wound; if it has pups, you have to call the vet and later advertise the pups for adoption. You cannot expect the young child whose puppy the dog originally was to attain the necessary wisdom overnight.

So to all those people who believe their child needs a pet, I would ask: do you yourselves want one? It's going to mean a lot of drudgery for you, not him. If the answer's yes, then a dog or a cat and, to a lesser extent, a guinea pig, goldfish, parakeet, rabbit or any of a dozen other kinds of animals are excellent for your child. Apart from providing companionship and entertainment, they will begin to teach him that someone else can depend on him. Remembering that "Spot" needs his dinner or that "Mitzi," the long-haired guinea pig, ought to be combed will develop a sense of responsibility in your child, not to mention bringing out such virtues in him as kindness, unselfishness, and gentleness.

Granted, some authorities claim that for young children to live in close proximity with animals is unhygienic. They could be right. I can only reply that my cat, my dog and my children all slept happily in the same room—even, I suspect, at times in the same bed—and nothing dreadful happened to any of them.

I admit that I couldn't always stop the dog from licking the three-year-old's face, but then Souha always took her duties seriously. On one memorable occasion my toddler decided to share a dog biscuit with Souha. Yet I'm still convinced that the advantages of having pets outweigh the slight risk of infection. One thing: my children all grew up fearless of animals. None of them ever dreaded a walk to the store in fear of encountering a strange dog, and that in itself is a boon.

If anything, I did a little too well in that direction. I once spent two hours sitting in a hospital with Merle waiting for an anti-tetanus injection. She had picked up a stray kitten, which in fright had ripped a piece of skin off her wrist. It wasn't her fault; on the contrary, she'd held the kitten the way we'd taught her. But nervous and unused to humans, it had scratched her in its attempt to escape.

So here endeth the first lesson: warn your child that strange animals are not necessarily as friendly as your own. Tell him never to approach a pet (especially a dog) that he doesn't know without first making sure it is agreeable. Show him how to offer the back of his hand for the dog to smell and accept, before he attempts to pat it. And if the dog is growling and jumping furiously, not to go up to it at all but to give it a wide berth.

Having decided to get a dog or cat, you come to the issue of the best age, from your child's viewpoint. (If you own a dog before you have your family, this question won't arise. You're unlikely to delay starting a baby for five years to accommodate your pet.) I would say not within the first nine months. At this stage perfect hygiene is vital (you should not have a crawling baby with an un-housebroken pup), and you have enough work what with the diapers and the 6 A.M. feeding without taking on any more.

My husband and I waited until Merle was two (and Tina, incidentally, eight) before we had Souha—a six-week-old shaggy sheepdog pup. And let me tell you: having two tots in the household (one two-legged and the other four-legged) is quite a merry-go-round. Typical of all young animals, Merle and Souha fought dozens of times a day. The puppy would grip the child's ankle sock with its teeth and hold on. Screams from the child. My husband Ian or I would rush to separate them, only to find two minutes later that the child had now seized the puppy's tail. Yelps from puppy.

However many times we separated them, however many times we punished the one who was inflicting the injury at the time, they always came together again. We couldn't turn our backs for five minutes. Then finally we found a simple expedient: every time there was a yelp from one or a scream from the other, we smacked both regardless—the hand and the snout. Within a week they were the best of friends, and never attacked one another again. So if you feel strong enough to buy a kitten or puppy while your child is still under three, I recommend that you try the same method of keeping the peace.

There's one thing to be said for putting up with a puppy and a toddler simultaneously: you get your reward when the next baby comes along. By then the dog is an adult. It's always lived with a child and so it isn't jealous of the new arrival—in fact, it is very often protective.

In our case, Souha was just over a year when Nicholas was born. She had watched our preparations for the new baby for many weeks, had looked curiously at the crib which was waiting, and finally had seen the baby lying in it. Nicholas was actually born in the hospital, but we came home within forty-eight hours. On the first morning, when the visiting nurse came to attend me and bathe the baby, something odd happened. The cot was between my bed and the wall, and when the nurse tried to slide it out, it wouldn't move. It appeared to be stuck. As she tugged and tugged, I glanced down—and saw Souha, usually friendly and docile, lying right across the bottom of the cot with her teeth bared a couple of inches from the nurse's ankle! I told the nurse to retreat and then passed the baby out to her. It seemed wiser to do that than to interfere with a dutiful sentry.

From that morning Souha was the best nursemaid I could have had. When the baby was out in his carriage, the dog sat beside it, on constant alert. If Nicholas so much as whimpered, in came Souha and nudged my leg until I went out to see what was wrong. I might add that no cat was foolish enough to venture within sight! And later on, the dog bore all sorts of pokings and pullings from Nicholas without a snarl; the greatest protest she ever registered was to walk away.

So a young, fully grown dog, between two and five, is probably the ideal if you have an infant. If you can't bear the pup idea, you could always take on someone else's older pet, or adopt one from such places as Bide-A-Wee.

What I would guard against is acquiring an old dog which has been totally unused to the wear and tear of young children. It might well be a little persnickety about rough handling. And when that happens, a pet is more of a worry than a joy.

Generally speaking, though, animals enrich a child's life, which is why a visit, or better still, a vacation, at a farm is so valuable. It always seems to me a lack that modern city children hardly know what cows, sheep, horses, pigs, donkeys, chickens, geese, and so forth look like, except from picture-books and on television. Living on a farm for a while and getting close to animals, watching them sleep and feed, and seeing horses groomed and cows milked . . . this is all part of the ever widening experience of life.

259

33

How Do I Tell My

Child About . . . ?

Children ask questions endlessly, especially those between two and five. Too young to be taught at school or to learn through reading, they badger their parents with "why's," because asking is a way of finding out.

I'm not talking about the "why" game—whatever reply Mother or Father gives, the child says: "Why?" It goes on and on until the parent, exasperated and exhausted, shouts "Because I say so!" That child doesn't even listen to the answers, he's merely clutching at attention.

No, I'm speaking of the genuine questions young children put to their parents, and what we, as adults, should tell them. I would tell the truth.

"Why can't we go shopping, Mommy?"

"Because the people who work in the stores have gone home, and the stores are closed."

"Why do we have to eat dinner?"

"Because eating helps us to grow and keep strong."

"Why is it dark at night?"

"Because we no longer face the sun."

"Is it night-time everywhere?"

"Well, no . . ." It's surprising what we as adults learn in answering our children correctly.

As a general rule, I would recommend that you answer only what is asked, because that's as much as the questioner can understand. If the child is capable of taking in more, or if your reply doesn't satisfy him, he will supply the rider question, like "Is it night-time everywhere?" If he still seems interested and you are tempted to elaborate, without prompting from him—well, communication between you never hurts. But don't kid yourself that you're teaching him anything further. You're not. It is only an older child who can grasp the extensions of a subject he's never even wondered about before.

Of course, if your under-five looks puzzled by your reply, that's as good as saying: "Hey, I don't get you; come again . . ." And in that case by all means try rephrasing your answer, but still only that one answer.

Let me warn you that you will be asked some things over and over again. That isn't due to forgetfulness on your child's part, but rather because the answer takes time to be absorbed. Stars aren't little lights, they're different suns.

Strange, that. Babies come from their mothers' bellies. Even more improbable—*he* came out of *yours*?

Sex

Mentioning pregnancy and birth leads me to say that there have always been "awkward" questions which young children ask, one of them being about sex. You will want to be prepared if the topic comes up in your household.

Let me say at the outset that, regrettably, children do not wait till a cozy autumn evening round the fire to ask "Mommy, where did I come from?" The topic is just as likely to arise in the line for the bus, where onlookers are bound to titter. But wherever your child asks the question, your answer should be the same: from my belly. Naturally, this is far easier for him to comprehend if you are pregnant. He sees your belly growing; toward the end of the nine months, he may even be able to feel the baby's movements. Even if you are not pregnant when he is between three and five, it is probable that a close friend of yours will be. So you can talk about the baby in her belly instead.

And contrary to what some people might believe, the fact that babies grow in their mothers' bellies may be all your child wants to know about the subject for the whole age-span of our book. If so, let him be. He'll get around to it again sometime in the future. (And it is just possible that he won't ask a thing about it.)

It is probable, however, that he'll want to know how

the baby got in your belly, in which case you say Daddy planted a seed, and the baby grew from that. You can illustrate this with the bulbs and seeds you plant in the yard, which grow into much bigger flowers. Another aspect that often worries children is how the baby is going to get out. To this, I've said "through a little tunnel between his mother's legs."

All right, you argue, they're the easy questions; how about the $64,000 one: *how* did Daddy plant this seed? Frankly, I've yet to meet a four-year-old who *volunteered* this question. But if yours does, then answer: "With his penis." If the truth is too absurd, too shattering for him to accept as yet, then he'll simply forget about it until he is ready. Don't be afraid that telling him about the sexual function of a penis is going to plague his mind with thoughts of Sin and Shame. This would happen only if your attitude when you spoke of sex was ashamed or salacious. Provided you remain matter-of-fact, so will your child. It is too early in his life to connect the making of babies with an expression of deep emotion.

If you are surprised or shocked that I should suggest using the word "penis" to a young child, I make no apology. I abhor cute names for the sexual organs. Moreover, I believe that automatically using the real ones eases discussion and attitudes about sex later on—in early adolescence and even in actual lovemaking. So I would suggest you teach your child the words "penis," "vagina," "testicles" as he or she needs the vocabulary.

This brings me to another tricky point. How does a little girl without a brother learn what a penis is? As I said earlier, I very much doubt if she'll care yet how that seed got inside. But if she does, there's always the hope that she'll have watched some baby boy relative or neighbor being bathed.

Or perhaps her daddy is one of those people who don't mind the family wandering in and out when he's sitting in the bath. If so, the problem is solved. But I am not for one moment suggesting that, for the sake of your children's sex education, you and your husband adopt standards which you consider immodest.

In the last decade or so, some experts have advocated nudity in the home because they believed it would prevent the next generation from growing up inhibited. And I'm sure it will, where parents treat it as a matter of course that their children will from time to time see them naked. But in families where the parents feel embarrassed about nudity but heroically strip anyway, it will have the reverse effect. The embarrassment transmits itself to the children, and they will grow up more inhibited than ever.

Conversely, too much flaunted liberalism over nudity can disturb a child. So I would say: stick to your own standards. If the worst comes to the worst, the brotherless little girl can always be told that a penis is rather like a finger, can't she?

What about the birds and the bees for sex education? Well, the reproduction of birds and bees is far too theoretical for an under-five, and it does presuppose that the parents are well-informed about the sex-life of the bee. But actually watching the birth of your dog's pups or the guinea pig next door having her babies—that's excellent for your child, an experience he will treasure.

Country children who have watched births and even matings ever since they can remember, almost always grow up with a healthy, natural attitude toward birth and sexual organs. They, of course, will have watched hundreds of young animals being suckled by their mothers.

And this is something that any town child can see as well—a cat nursing her kittens, a monkey at the zoo with her newborn baby. Take every opportunity of pointing this out to your child, and explain that this is the way the mother feeds her baby: from her own body. It is even better, of course, if your child can watch you breast-feeding his younger brother or sister. Or perhaps you have a friend who *honestly* wouldn't mind him watching her nurse. The more he can learn about sex as he learns about everything else, the better.

Talking to Strangers

How do you warn your children against talking to the wrong kind of strangers? If you abide by my rule of not letting your child wander about on his own, the chances of his talking to someone he should not are limited, aren't they? Even so, I know that there are occasions when one parent out of a group goes down to the park or playground or nursery school to escort all the children home, and this would be an opportunity on which a stranger could step in and pose as "the person Mommy sent."

How do you guard against such a thing? First, you promise your child that you will never ever send someone he doesn't know as your ambassador; second, you instill in him from the first time he plays outside that he must not under any circumstances speak to strangers or take candy or money from them. (You needn't frighten him with reasons. The under-five has to take an awful lot of rules on your say-so.) To underline this point, I have even handed back chocolates elderly ladies kindly offered my own children in the park. "I'm afraid they're not allowed to accept candy from strangers," I explained. "But thank you all the same."

Adoption

If your child is adopted, I don't think you can do better than the well-tried method of telling him a story of how you came to choose him. It should be among the first stories you tell your child and it will become such a favorite you will probably have to repeat it time and time again. "Once upon a time Mommy and Daddy were lonely because they had no little boy or girl to live with them. So they went to a big white stone house where there were a lot of children who had no mothers and fathers."

Elaborate on the story; take it slowly. Tell how the nurse in charge took you into a big room full of cribs, and in

266

the fourth crib was a lovely little boy. And he smiled at you, and you both smiled back. And then you played peekaboo together, and you loved each other very much. And you were allowed to take him home. "And that little boy was *you*." As he grows older, you can go into even more details about your journey home, and how he first saw his own room, and what Teddy thought of him when they said "hello."

But don't fall into the trap of suggesting you chose him because he was pretty, or because you wanted a brother for your own daughter, or because he was a new baby. You chose him because he was himself. And however it may have started out, now you do love him for himself, don't you?

Later on, of course, he is going to ask what happened to his real Mommy. Don't be hurt by this question. He asks it because he is curious, not because he loves you less. He deserves an honest answer—as honest as is possible without wounding him. "She died." Or "She didn't have a Daddy to help her look after you, and so she asked the nurse in the big white house to find you a Mommy and Daddy, and we loved you so much she picked us."

It's strange, but although a child adopted as a baby can't remember his natural parents and therefore can have no love for them, the biological link, particularly with the mother, is so strong that to learn he was *deserted* can have serious psychological repercussions. That's why an adopted child can usually accept that his real mother died (because she had no choice about leaving him), but not that she abandoned him at a church door.

267

While speaking of the adopted child, may I put in a plea not to overcompensate for the deprivation of his natural parents? You are already giving him what he needs most in the world: the deep love you would give a son or daughter you had conceived yourselves. So once you have adopted a child, treat him as your own. Smack him when he's spiteful; deny him candy that would harm his teeth; refuse to sit by his crib all evening. In other words, let him grow up into a reasonable human being.

Death

What you tell your child about what happens to people when they die will depend largely on your own religious beliefs—or absence of them. If you believe your late mother has gone to heaven, then that is what you say. A three- or four-year-old will be satisfied to learn Grandma has gone to a peaceful other world. If you don't accept any form of life after death, then I would suggest you describe Grandma as having gone to sleep forever. Your child will have seen old people sleeping in their chairs, babies in their carriages, perhaps even Daddy on a Sunday morning—and he will know it's a quiet, relaxed state to be in.

In any event, I think children should be told when a member of their family has died. Death is a sad subject, but it's one we all have to learn to accept.

If there is a dead bird on the lawn, don't pretend it's invisible. You should tell your child calmly and sympathetically that the bird has died because there's been a week of snow and no food for it. And later you discreetly dispose of the corpse. If your dog kills a rabbit, explain to your child that dogs, left wild and living without a family to feed them dog-food, eat rabbits to live. Cats kill birds, but in turn birds eat worms. Young children are not so appalled by the cruelty of nature as one might think. Sometimes, though, they do go through a morbid phase, when for weeks on end they keep asking you about death. If your child reacts in this way, don't be alarmed; it's one of those subjects that takes a lot of absorbing.

Finally, I would say that it is a mistake to let your child see the body of someone dear to him who has died. It is far better for him to remember that person as he or she was.

I would extend that to cover very sick people. By all means, let the child send messages, or even better a painting or gift he has made, but don't inflict on him visits that could frighten or depress him.

Separation or Divorce

There is no painless way of telling a child that his mother or father will not be living with him any more. But at least you can stop the knife from going in even deeper; don't say that "Daddy has *left* us." As I said when talking about adoption, children cannot bear to have been deserted by their parents. So however bitter you may feel about the break-up of your marriage, try to reassure your child that Daddy still loves him. He has gone away only because he couldn't be happy living in this house with you both. (Say this even if it isn't the whole truth, in order to persuade him his father loves him.) And wherever possible, permit your child to continue to have some sort of relationship with his absent parent.

Remarriage?

Introducing a stepmother or stepfather into the home is never simple, admittedly, but I don't believe it is quite so difficult as the romantic novels would have us believe. Their idea of Father going away to Spain for the summer and returning with a beautiful bride whom the children have never seen doesn't happen in real life—or at least I hope it doesn't. In practice, surely, the children already know Helen. She's a friend who visits, who helps bathe them before she and Daddy go out for the evening, who cooked for them at Christmas. If this isn't the case, it ought to be, before the day that Daddy tells his children that Helen is coming to live with them permanently. Or, in the case of a stepfather, he has played ball with them, he has taken them on automobile trips, he has answered their questions.

The point I'm making is that Helen or Joe are friends of the children, quite apart from their relationship with the parent. And that is how I think they should approach their new role after the wedding-day as well: as a friend, not as a substitute Mommy or Daddy. I believe that much of the resentment over stepmothers and stepfathers can be put

270

down to the children's feeling that Helen or Joe are usurping a position held by someone very dear to them. It might even be better if the children called them "Helen" or "Joe" rather than "Mommy" or "Daddy." In fact, I know of a delightful instance where the stepmother was called by her given name to start with, but after a year or so she became "Mommy" instead. Nobody suggested the change, and it wasn't even a conscious one. She had simply grown into her new title.

To potential step-parents, I would say: don't expect to love your fiancé's children as you would your own. Like them as people in their own right, not only as an adjunct of your beloved. And once married, don't be so anxious to please the children that you allow yourself to be an overindulgent parent. A step-parent must assume all the responsibilities of parenthood—protection, correction, and attention. Remember, we are talking in this book of children under five.

If you really cannot abide your fiancé's child or, as happens more often, your child hates your intended (probably due to jealousy), I would strongly advise you to postpone your wedding until the relationship improves. Let the potential step-parent and the child spend time alone together. For instance, a game of football for "the men" might just do the trick. And if at the end of, say, a year, the situation is no better, then I would seriously reconsider whether this marriage is right for you. Taking sides in a war between your husband and your child—or being the cause of one between your new wife and her jealous little son—will tear you apart.

271

34

It's a Date!

Every so often in family life there are special occasions—
dates you note down in your diary and plan for weeks
ahead. Some of these dates should include your child—his
birthday party would be rather pointless without him!—but
some of them shouldn't. I feel that children under five do
not belong at Grandpa's and Grandma's twenty-fifth anni-
versary dinner, or at young Aunt Ida's wedding reception.
They get in the way, turning a festive day or evening into a
nightmare of "Don't touch those flowers, Susie" and
"Johnnie, stop playing tag around the table." So don't drag
your child along to get bored, frustrated, and upset. Leave
him home with a sitter.

And on the subject of weddings, think twice about being flattered into letting your little girl be a bridesmaid. The six- to ten-year-olds adore the long dresses and all the fuss, but the two-, three-, or four-year-old will at best become overexcited at all the attention, and at worst will howl.

The Christening

Probably, though, the first date in your child's social diary will not be a wedding, but his own christening.

I must say right off that I'm a firm believer in total religious freedom. It is not my business to advocate or condemn christening in principle. But for the sake of the people who do have their children christened, I would be shirking my obligation if I didn't comment at all.

Now, it seems to me that the religious service and the social gathering that goes with a christening have become almost inseparable, and I fear this is not good. The Victorian photograph of Grandma gliding down the staircase in her trailing dress, carrying the new baby in his best robe, looks romantic and charming. But Grandma had servants to help her with the preparations, and a nurse standing by to remove the infant at the auspicious moment. Nowadays, when few of us can afford cooks and nursemaids—or can find them if we can afford them—and have to get up ourselves at 2 A.M. for the night-feeding, the grand manner doesn't come easily.

When I suggested to a young mother that giving an enormous party within two months of childbirth was perhaps rash because she didn't have all her strength back, she said in a shocked voice, "But the party's not for my benefit; it's for the baby's!"

Hmmm. I have yet to meet the baby who enjoyed his christening party. In my experience, every baby has found it upsetting, and it stands to reason. Lunch comes up early because he has to be at the church by 11 o'clock; his afternoon rest doesn't materialize for hours because of all the guests around, and dinner is late because Mother is a bit woozy from all those champagne toasts. The people about are all strange, making a lot of noise and smoking . . . and, worst of all, peering at him. And if he is being breast-fed, he won't appreciate the decrease in his milk supply due to his mother's nervous tension and fatigue.

But aren't we stuck with the christening in its present form? No, say I, not if we're of a mind to rebel. If it's a question of aunts and friends wanting "to see the baby," invite them round in twos and threes for a cup of tea and some cookies. That way they and the baby will have a chance to become properly acquainted as individuals. I realize that a daytime get-together generally has to exclude the menfolk, but it's a rare man who wants to see someone else's new baby.

As for the christening ceremony, well, you don't *need* dozens of onlookers there either—just the three of you and the godparents and grandparents if they want to come. And your child does not have to be christened while he's still a babe-in-arms, anyway. My own eldest wasn't christened until she was four, and I think she benefited from the delay. Tina attended Sunday school, and, on learning that all the other boys and girls there had been "christened," she asked to be christened, too. Because she was old enough to understand what was going on and because it was by her own choice, the service meant a great deal more to her. Moreover, the Sunday school teachers used the service to demonstrate the religious meaning of christening to the rest of the school.

The First Birthday

But if you christen your child early, as most people do, the next big occasion on his calendar is his first birthday.

Yes, I know many young parents make much of their offspring's first birthday. They buy a cake with one candle on it, they invite other children, along with *their mothers* . . .

Do you seriously imagine that a one-year-old enjoys such a party? If he is in a good mood that day, he might accept it. But if he's tired or crotchety or teething, then he's going to be upset by all the commotion, by the highly suspect presence of other babies, and by his mother's preoccupation with the entertaining. Thus he's the person who least enjoys his birthday party. All his parents have achieved is to have kept up with the Joneses, who had a birthday party for their one-year-old.

How much better for your family to celebrate the day

quietly. There is a whole lifetime for big, noisy parties, when your child will be able to handle his role as host. So this year let him spend it just with you, with Father if possible, and with his older brothers and sisters, who for once should be encouraged to put themselves out for the birthday child. As for three or four other guests: they should be his friends—adults with endless patience for ball rolling and knee bouncing.

And believe me: your baby's stomach is far safer with a little treat like a chocolate cookie and a little ice cream than with a tableful of sweet stuff. Moreover, he'd rather have you playing with him on the floor than dashing about being a hostess.

I've said it a dozen times: the young child needs time to appreciate things—the candle on his cake, a new toy he's been given (and I'd suggest you space out his presents, because a whole slew of them will only confuse him), and his pretty cards. Incidentally, if you've the sort of child who genuinely likes looking at pictures and carting them about, then I'd allow him to play with his birthday cards. After all, they were sent for his pleasure, not just to be displayed on the mantelpiece.

The Second and Third Birthdays

Almost all of what I've just said applies equally to Birthday No. 2. By then, your child may well appreciate friends of his own age, but, much as he'd miss them if he couldn't play

276

with them ordinarily, I doubt if he'll welcome them on *his* day. I suspect his idea of bliss is to have all his new toys to himself, to have the undistracted attention of Mother, and to eat a plate of ice cream in his own chair. Two-year-olds, remember, are famous for their tantrums; in a party atmosphere, you're bound to spark off at least one of them.

On his third birthday your child might indeed enjoy having a small party. He won't like forty small guests (thank heaven). He won't even like fourteen. But half a dozen other children between three and five will probably please him a lot. Invite children he knows well and likes; otherwise shyness or tears may ruin the party. So ask his young cousin, the little boy across the street, a friend's daughter with whom he always plays happily and, if he attends nursery school, his closest pals from there.

You may have to ask the women who run the school who those pals are, because children under five never mention Best Friend Simon's existence. And needless to say, *you*, not your child, must speak to Simon's mother, not to Simon. If you leave it to the boys, Simon may show up the same day he's invited or never show up at all.

By the way, a good idea for children who attend nursery school is to hold the party at milk-and-cookie time at school. *You* provide sandwiches and cake and balloons and whistles and the teacher provides control. It's a good idea because you share the festivity with your child without having to worry about the mechanics of the party. What's more, your child's guests are all the small people with whom he's learning to form relationships on a regular basis. And best of all, for you and for the mothers of your child's schoolmates, you don't have to have a whole flock of other mothers on hand.

If you do have to have the party at home (and presumably, even though he has his school party, he will want some sort of celebration with his family), don't let the adults around take over the day. I appreciate that many three-year-olds cannot adjust happily to unfamiliar surroundings unless their mothers are there, so you may have to invite some parents. Just be sure the occasion remains "child-oriented"—i.e., that their party doesn't become your coffee-klatsch.

The Fourth and Fifth Birthdays

For the fourth birthday and finally for the fifth, I'd make a rule: no mothers. By now your child will want about ten guests, and that's quite enough without ten adults as well. Granted, you're going to need help. But I think it's better if your ally "behind the lines" in the kitchen and "at the front" in the games room isn't one of the other children's mothers. This mother's child is likely to be embarrassed by her presence and show off, which will add to your trouble, not lessen it.

Naturally, Father is the perfect choice . . . but only if Father honestly wants to be there. Most fathers, however devoted they may be, detest children's parties. So if you're not lucky enough to be married to one of the rare saints, give in gracefully. Take it from one who knows. If your husband shudders at the very idea of organizing a game of musical chairs, he is better off out of the way. You and a friend will get on faster without him.

Doing what? Supervising and organizing, organizing, organizing. If your party invitations state *"from 3 o'clock till six,"* allow forty minutes for eating and fill most of the rest of the time with organized games. If the party's in the summer and you're fortunate enough to have a yard with play equipment in it—sand-pit, paddling pool, swing, climbing-frame, tent, tricycle—or a lawn large enough for a ball game, you're home free, practically. All you will have to do is stay around with a hawk's eye and a first-aid kit. But if your party is to be held indoors and you leave the children to amuse themselves, anarchy will reign. They need to be told what to do; they need the security of knowing someone bigger than they are is in charge.

Party Games

There are a number of books on the market which describe games suitable for different age-groups, including three-to-five-year-olds. If their suggestions don't inspire you, perhaps the best person to consult would be the nursery school teacher.

There are certain basic favorites, but I think every party should have at least one original game as well. Whatever is played, though, keep it simple. I've seen high-I.Q. adults baffled by the rules of a new game as

279

described by their hostess (and three other people simultaneously), so take pity on an under-five.

And do remember that the attention-span of three-to-five-year-olds is short. Almost any game that lasts longer than ten minutes should be ruled out before you begin, because some of your guests will become bored by it and quit. You will then have a rival faction amusing itself while you are desperately trying to maintain the official program. This can also happen with elimination games—the ones who are out grow bored just watching. Before they begin jumping from chair to chair, see that your second in command is keeping them busy.

If you decide to award prizes for the games, then it is your job as the host's adult representative to ensure that every child wins something. The child whose pin comes nearest to the donkey's tail is an undisputed winner, but it's easy to "fix" such competitions as musical chairs so that the winner is someone else. Bend backward and sideways to make sure that no child, even your own, is left out. I know your own child has already received X number of presents, but a prize is something to be proud of.

All children love to have something to show off at home. So, I fear you'll have to distribute some loot. It needn't be expensive—wax crayons, plastic cars, or even just balloons. But make much of the giving. Have the gifts drawn from a big pot or a tub, or handed out, if the party occurs around Christmas time, by a dressed-up Santa Claus.

As for the catering, Think Disposable and avert breakage and dishwashing. These days the paper mugs, plates, and napkins often look nicer than the real thing anyway. And if you're holding the party at a nursery school, throw-away crockery solves a transport problem.

Party Food

With regard to the food itself, always bear in mind that young children are the most conservative of eaters. "What's *that?*" they say, turning up their noses at anything unfamiliar. So now is not the time for avocado salad. What I've found goes down well is familiar foods in unfamiliar guises, and small amounts at a time—for instance, sausages, cubes of cheese and pineapple, and pieces of ham on cocktail toothpicks. Another good idea is crackers, thinly spread with butter, with cheese or chicken on top. And in summer, nothing is more appetizing than a dish of red baby tomatoes which a child can pop in his mouth whole, or scrubbed new miniature carrots. Potato chips, salted peanuts, and pretzels will vanish fast.

Passing on to the next course, as it were . . . ice cream is a must. And almost all children of this age like Jell-O, so it helps if the Jell-O is in small, individual bowls of paper or plastic, ready. It's one less serving job to do during the devouring session. If you think Jell-O on its own is a bit dull—and I must confess I do—add fresh or tinned fruit.

Beware, though, of doing something fancy with the minor pastry. In the past, I've spent an hour baking chocolate cupcakes, only to have them regarded with

281

suspicion by Merle's friends, and finally to be asked for the store-bought brand they recognized.

And to drink, I don't think you can do better than colas and soda pops. Yes, I know I said I wasn't in favor of them, but this is a *birthday*, for heaven's sake!

And lastly we come to the Birthday Cake. By now nearly all the children will be too full to eat any and, besides, many of them find the traditional cake too rich. That's why I'd go instead for a chocolate sponge with cream in it. The candles—to be blown out to a quavering chorus of "Happy Birthday"—look just as good on that. But if you really do fancy cake with icing, be prepared to wrap the pieces in napkins for your small guests to take home to their mothers.

Before I leave food, let me issue a warning. Children don't eat a quarter of what you assume they will. Don't overcater: it will break your heart.

Ending a party is as difficult as starting one. You don't want to have the children just sitting around, bored, waiting to be collected. And on the other hand, it's unfair to play a wildly stimulating game from which their mothers will have to drag them away. If your budget permits, the ideal is a hired magician or ventriloquist for twenty minutes or so: or if you have a movie projector, a short cartoon film.

But if these ideas are far too extravagant, then a fitting end to a very nice day would be to read a story from a new book your child's been given. Once again, your extra adult is valuable: if she reads the story, then you're free to answer the door to the mothers and perhaps give them a cup of tea and a piece of cake.

For the moment of parting, your child should be taught the social graces of saying "Thank you for coming to my party," just as his guest should say "Thank you for having me." Incidentally, when your child is a guest at a party, don't ever humiliate him by arriving late to collect him. If the invitation said *"6 o'clock,"* be there at six, having allowed for the traffic jam or the missed bus. Don't make him sit there all alone looking abandoned.

35

Christmas with the Children

Christmas with children in the house is wonderful. At the risk of sounding sentimental for once, the peaceful, sophisticated Christmases my family enjoys now are certainly not so exhausting as they used to be, but they're not so much fun. So appreciate this decade or so of family Christmases, tiring though they are, while you may. They won't last forever. But don't imagine that these joyous Yuletides start the moment you have a baby.

I repeat again, babies like familiarity and routine—and the 24th, 25th, and 26th of December are to them just three more days. Certainly with the baby of under a year, you should aim to keep the part of the day when he's up and about as quiet and as close to an ordinary Saturday as possible.

Even when he's over a year, take it easy. He can't comprehend what Christmas is all about, and the tense excitement and noise could distress him. And don't be surprised if he plays with the fancy wrappings and the boxes with great glee, but ignores the presents that came in them. That's typical.

By all means, give your child a turkey dinner in gravy with a potato and perhaps two or three sprouts, but lay off the cranberry sauce and the plum pudding, or he'll pay you back by crying all evening with a stomach-ache.

The Tree

As your child grows out of babyhood, Christmas becomes a day on which things are exciting, although he doesn't quite understand why. He knows only that it's something to look forward to. He knows the day is nearing when Father brings in a tree and hangs colored lights and bubbles and tinsel on it to make it bright and pretty. (Even a young baby will watch the lights flickering on and off.)

But the tree's very attraction spells danger to a young child. Unless the tree is well out of his reach, behind some kind of barrier or up high, your child may well grasp one of the glass balls and hurt himself—or pull the whole tree over and hurt you.

I'm against letting a child under five help hang the decorations, both on the tree and around the room, because it's a long job (it always takes us more hours than we allow), and he'll soon get bored. He'll twist up the scotch tape you asked him to hold and kick at the holly-wreath lying on the floor, he'll play with the scissors and empty the pin box—and you'll wind up cursing Christmas, your child and any merry gentleman who is foolish enough to put his head through the doorway.

So I would suggest you decorate after your child is in bed, and then watch his face next morning when he comes down to find the living room transformed into fairyland.

Santa Claus

As for Santa Claus . . . Now I know that he has nothing to do with the birth of Christ, that pretending he exists is lying to your child, that his jolly figure commercializes and debases Christmas—but I like Santa Claus. In our family he always left a stocking at the foot of the bed and drank the milk the children left out for him. The stockings contained only trifles—a doll's-house bed, a bar of chocolate, crayons, a plastic car, a tangerine, a yo-yo—but they made a heap of bounty to a waking child.

After breakfast the children were allowed to unwrap all the presents sent by friends who would not be spending the holiday with us. These were quite definitely from Jean and Peter or Mr. and Mrs. Bloggs, and not from Santa Claus. We explained that this was the Season of Goodwill, and that people expressed their goodwill toward each other

286

by giving presents. At the same time this system got round the awkward problem of Mr. and Mrs. B. expecting to be thanked for their gifts and the child not appreciating it was from them. Then from unwrapping time till lunch, I do not think it's unreasonable for any child to play with his new toys or his Dad while Mother gets on with the cooking.

After lunch in our home came the big ceremony of family present-giving. These were either handed round by the youngest children or by Santa Claus, some well-intentioned male relative or friend who had been bribed to don a false beard and red suit and carry a sack loaded with gifts. If the children half-recognized Uncle Tom, they didn't let on. In fact my children told me only recently how they kept it from us for a couple of years that they no longer believed in Santa Claus. They thought we'd be disappointed. They were right. Christmas never was quite the same without Santa Claus.

What Not to Give

What Christmas presents should be depends, of course, on the tastes of your child, but I can suggest a few things they *shouldn't* be. Perhaps if I list some of the mistakes Ian and I and other parents have made, it might save you and your child from disappointment.

A rocking horse superbly carved and complete with leather saddle and reins may look very impressive to an adult, but there isn't much a three- or four-year-old can use

287

it for. He or she isn't old enough for imaginative cowboy and fairy-tale prince games that require a saddle horse. On the other hand, he's outgrown such passive entertainment as mounting and rocking for hours on end.

A similar error is the large, beautifully dressed doll. A child will press her nose to the shop-window and beg you to buy it for her. But once she owns it, she finds there's nothing she can do with it *but* admire it . . . and that much she could have done from outside the shop. She can't wash its clothes, she can't pin up its hair; it's so obviously a "lady" doll that it's impossible to pretend it could be her baby. (But she may appreciate such a doll in later years.)

One Christmas we saved up hard to buy Merle a huge brown bear, almost as tall as she was. We imagined it would be a real companion for her. It proved much too overpowering to be a friend; it was just a big static object. I would never make that sort of mistake again.

In the same way, an animal that is too faithful a reproduction of an animal—you know, on all fours and without the big-eyed trimmings and floppy ears that make soft toys appealing—can't be treated as another small human. I remember when a polar bear was born at the zoo near us, somebody brought out a perfect—and costly—toy version of her. Some people I knew bought one for their three-year-old daughter. She never played with it. She couldn't think of any games with a cast of one little girl and one polar bear.

Despite the old joke, I doubt that any father has ever bought his one-week-old son a set of electric trains. But I've heard of one or two who've bought their *three*-year-olds

288

train sets, complete with freight yards, switches, viaducts, and heaven knows what. Now, if Father wants a train set that badly for Christmas, I don't see why he shouldn't have one, and then his young son can play with him for as long as it interests the child. But don't let's pretend the train set is a gift to anyone except Father. It's the same with the full-size football ostensibly for the two-year-old. It's too big for the toddler and Father feels disappointed because he has to play all by himself.

Seriously, with the best intentions, one can waste an awful lot of money. The under-five is delightfully *un*materialistic; he doesn't appreciate something just because it cost a lot of money. A little girl of four-and-a-half once told me that her "best" presents were her skipping rope (which didn't cost a dollar) and her doll's carriage (which cost $30) in that order.

So the rocking horse, the big bear, the dressed doll, the football, lie ignored in a corner, while your child plays with the stuffed elephant the old lady next door knitted for him.

And this is the moment to hide away some of the discarded toys. Most children get far more presents at Christmas than they can cope with. They unwrap each parcel, look at it, handle it, but as the mountain grows, they don't really take in what the gift is. I've often seen my own children reach the stage where they're holding one thing in their hand while trying to open the next one. So when the present-opening is at last over and your child is absorbed in showing off his new scooter, scoop up half of the barely acknowledged gifts and put them away in a box upstairs.

Between Christmas and spring there are going to be an

awful lot of days when he can't play outside because it's sleeting, or when he's ill with a cold and needs cheering up, or when he's just plain fed up with everything he owns. On those occasions you will be glad you have a box of "new" toys upstairs to amuse him. Don't produce the boxful, though—get out one or two things. And it's surprising, now that he has the time to study it, how fascinating Aunt Mary's puzzle will appear to him.

Before I leave the subject of Christmas, I ought to warn you about the well-meaning relative who gives your child a bag of sweets all to himself. A quarter-pound of chocolate might please him very much, but on Christmas Day it is also likely to make him sick. I cannot emphasize enough that children under five should not be given rich, exotic foods or sips from the wine-glasses of everybody in the room. Your *child* might tolerate the strange tastes very happily, but his digestive system won't. Nor, I suspect, will ours, but we're too old to learn.

36

When Your Child Is Ill

According to Mary Poppins, a spoonful of sugar helps the medicine go down. My spoonful of sugar comes in extra glucose for energy, extra loving attention for comfort, and well-beloved old toys for diversion.

How do you know when your child is not well? When a normally happy and active child becomes listless and fretful and loses interest in his surroundings—this is often the first sign that he's coming down with something. Since a baby or toddler can't tell you where it hurts, you have to investigate. First take his temperature. Put him on your lap and soothe him—it's difficult to keep the thermometer in place if a child is struggling and protesting.

Do not take his temperature anywhere except in the groin. The mercury bulb has to lie next to the skin in the fold between his torso and his thigh, and be kept there for two full minutes by your watch. I've found the easiest way to do this is by crossing his knees and pressing your hand firmly against the thigh. If his temperature is slightly above 99° F., then he is probably only in for a cold. If it's above 101°, inform your doctor immediately. And if it's 95° or below, and the child's skin feels cold and clammy, also tell your doctor.

Check for rashes. See whether his nose is so blocked that he'd have trouble eating and drinking. Listen for the barking cough of croup. Vomiting and diarrhea together, particularly in a very young baby, signal danger that requires urgent medical attention. Ear-discharge and ear-ache, undue coughing, or belly-ache also indicate that something is seriously amiss. I hardly need mention that a child who has fits or convulsions, or who has swallowed something like a penny, a pin or the pills you didn't lock up safely, needs a doctor at once.

Don't Play Doctor

It is wrong to try to diagnose your child's illness and to treat him yourself without medical advice. The important thing is to inform your doctor what the symptoms are, and to let him decide whether you should take the child to the office. (It's not a good thing to cart your baby or toddler to a crowded waiting room, especially when he's ill. I believe doctors should make house calls, but few of them do anymore.) The doctor may instruct you over the telephone, which is fine; but carry out those instructions conscientiously and call him back when asked to or if your child's condition gets worse.

Ideally, you should call your doctor during his office hours, preferably in the daytime. It is rare that a child's illness, except if it is a sudden emergency, starts after midnight, but many doctors complain that they get calls at 1 A.M. about children who have been ill since lunch. So phone your doctor when you first *think* you may need his help—not at 2 o'clock in the morning, when you are *sure* you do.

If you can't reach your doctor and he hasn't responded within four or five hours to the messages you've left, call the nearest hospital or your volunteer ambulance corps. Or perhaps your town has a Save-A-Life League which keeps in contact with available doctors twenty-four hours a day, just for emergencies. If you're new in town, inquire about the League—whose service is free—and keep its phone number by your telephone.

Never give a child medicines prescribed or bought for someone else, or even the remainder of those prescribed for him on a previous occasion. When your doctor gives you a new prescription, have it filled as soon as possible—not ten hours later when your husband comes home. If you can't leave the house, ask your doctor to phone the prescription to the druggist.

Carry out dosage instructions precisely. Twice the dose

in half the time won't make your child better twice as fast; it could make him a lot sicker. Don't stop the treatment just because your child seems a bit better. If the doctor said he needs a full bottle of medicine, then that's what he needs . . . even if it takes him an additional four days after he's fit to finish it up.

Convalescent Hygiene

Apart from any specific instructions the doctor gives, I recommend that any child with a temperature of more than 100° F. be kept in bed. But that's no reason for not maintaining hygiene. In illnesses accompanied by fever, it is important to keep him clean and his *teeth brushed.*

Before bathing a sick child in his bed, make sure the room is good and warm. Warm a pair of fresh pajamas and a towel. Cover the bed or crib with a waterproof sheet, then cover this with a spare blanket. Put the child on top, and cover him with a second spare blanket. (Spare blankets too must be warmed after a good airing.) Have a basin of warm water ready and a baby-bath disinfecting solution instead of soap. Your doctor will have to give you a prescription for the solution; federal regulations no longer permit its unrestricted sale and use on babies.

Take off the child's pajamas under the blanket, wash a small part of his body, and dry it. Only expose the part you are washing, not the whole child. When you have finished, whisk out the spare blankets and waterproof cover, dress

294

the child in clean warm pajamas, and tuck him up again.

I think it's worth mentioning that for colds or other respiratory infections, you can help drain the child's air passages if you tip the crib or bed at the foot end. A pair of ordinary bricks placed lengthwise, one under each leg, serves admirably. This means that the child's feet are about four inches higher than his head. Have a pad on the head-end of the crib so the child won't bump his head.

Amusements

Now, I know from experience, and I'm sure you do too, that when one is ill one gets thoroughly bored with lying in bed and looking at the walls for days on end. For this reason, I suggest that during the day your sick child be nursed on a bed made up with sheets and blankets on the living-room sofa. He can be moved to his own bedroom at his usual bedtime. His bedroom can be aired while he's out of it, and his bed will then be fresh and much nicer to spend the night in. Apart from its being a change to come to the living room, he has the advantage of your company; he can watch all the other activities that go on there, and watch television.

Unlike adult patients, children don't knit, read, or do cross-word puzzles, but they do need to play and have things to do. It would be rare that a child who is allowed to be nursed at home is so ill that he hasn't the energy to sit up and play in his sickbed. First of all, his usual bed-companions will be welcome and, oddly enough, he will often prefer an old, much-used, no longer smart rabbit to a new friend he got for his birthday. No adult chooses the moment when he has a raging temperature to conquer Sartre. So with a child—he does not want games that challenge him; he wants a puzzle he can solve, a castle he can build, a picture-book he knows by heart. So fish out the toys you thought he'd outgrown a year ago.

Many games need a flat, hard surface, so he'll probably need a tray. An even better piece of equipment is a cantilever-table. I've got one myself, and apart from finding it mighty useful when nursing my family, it makes a luxurious bedside-table for guests or a super breakfast-table for a spoiled husband.

Take convalescence gently. Your child should not be up until his temperature is back to normal and then only for half a day at first. Dress him properly when he first gets up again—the floor may be drafty. Don't take him out for a walk until he has been up for a normal day, and watch the weather. Overdressing a child in warm weather is as detrimental as underdressing him in the winter.

One more thing: In the interest of good discipline, gradually withdraw any special privileges of sickness during convalescence—otherwise they'll become bad habits.

37

Accidents—Better Safe

than Sorry

Of the thousands of accidental deaths at home each year, a great number are of children under five.

While your children are small, you must be on constant alert. If the house has been suspiciously peaceful for the last ten minutes, find out why. Remember that between the ages of eighteen months and four years, a child is adventurous and curious, but he has little if any prudence. He knows how to stand on a chair and reach up to things, but doesn't understand the possible results. He will be able to open the front gate, but he will not realize the dangers beyond.

I'd be the last person to recommend that you sit there considering every crisis that could occur. Only by wrapping

297

your child in cotton batting can you protect him from every danger, and that would bring its own problems. My point is: don't ask for trouble. And as your child's comprehension increases, explain to him why he mustn't do certain things. But to start with, you won't be able to reason with him at all. So let's begin with Safety First for a baby.

Baby Equipment

You can prevent some accidents before he's born. Check that the equipment you buy him—his crib, his playpen, his baby chair—meet safety standards. This will assure, for example, that his head won't jam between bars or his high chair collapse when he leans back. Take added care when selecting his carriage. By all means fall in love with a yellow one, if you wish, but before signing the check, walk round the store a bit with the carriage. If the handle is at an uncomfortable height for you, you run the risk of leaning on it too heavily and tipping it over. That also happens to mothers who hang shopping-bags over the handle, or sling a bag over an arm that holds the carriage; it upsets the balance. The proper place to put things when shopping is a tray underneath the carriage's chassis. Look for a carriage that has one—unless you shop by car.

If you're a half-pint, be sure you can see over the hood when it's up. Pay special attention to the brake. Would you trust it on an incline in wet, slippery weather? If the answer's no, I'd find another carriage. A good brake is imperative, and you should use it even when you've only stopped to fish out your plastic rain hat.

If the carriage is of the kind that can be taken apart for travel or storage, take a tip from a young mother I know: Don't trust the salesman's word that the chassis comes off in three seconds. Try it, in the shop, even if other customers are waiting. Make sure you can do it in a reasonable time. It isn't much good that your husband can bat the chassis into position if he's going to be away at work when you need to get the two halves in and out of the car. And to use the carriage incorrectly assembled, wobbling somewhere around the middle, could have hideous consequences.

Finally, check that the carriage has sensible anchor points for a harness. I've seen poor babies pinned like butterflies on a board because their harness rings were in the wrong position. And having got the rings for a harness, buy him the harness. (Leather ones look grand, but plain ordinary webbing generally proves more comfortable.) That carriage is a long way up; your baby really does need to be strapped in. Loosening one side of the harness to give him more freedom is almost worse than no harness at all: if he did fall, he'd be left hanging.

Another sensible safety measure is to buy a net for the carriage. It will protect baby against insects, birds, and toddlers' curious fingers.

Never push a baby carriage out into the street from between parked vehicles or at a curve, and then peer out yourself to see if the coast is clear. If a car had been coming, the carriage would have already been hit. Another thing: before you had the baby, you may have been awfully agile about dodging through moving traffic. With a baby carriage, don't try it. It's a big, long thing, not easy to maneuver quickly—and your precious baby is in it. I know it's a bore, but cross only at pedestrian crossings—and only with the traffic light.

Choking

Earlier, we discussed the need for sterilization to kill germs. But infection isn't the only danger connected with feeding. Of all fatal accidents in the home, the greatest killer among babies is choking. The majority are victims of propped-up bottles, but some merely throw up in their cribs, cannot yet turn away, inhale the vomit, and choke. Frightening thought. But the risk is almost nullified if you always lay baby on his side or stomach . . . not on his back.

If your baby is choking, the first thing to do is to hook out with your finger whatever is obstructing his throat. Then hold him upside down by his ankles with one hand, and give several firm thumps between his shoulders with the other.

Scalding

Another point about feeding: you can bet your life that if you ever forget to carry out the wrist-test on his milk, that'll be the occasion when it will be too hot and will scald his mouth. Solution: don't forget. Always check that a liquid is no more than body temperature before your baby tells you it isn't.

The other time-proven test is the elbow one for bath-water. Well, before you decide that that's far too tepid a temperature and run in an extra couple of gallons of hot water (always, incidentally, put the cold water in first), just test your own bath-water the same way. You'll begin to agree that your hands are considerably less sensitive, and less reliable as a thermometer, than the rest of your body.

Even in the best regulated homes, young children do get scalded. Here's what to do about it. Forget the outdated butter routine, and for that matter any other creams. Plain cool water's the thing. The aim is to reduce the skin temperature, and the fastest way of doing that is to immerse the damaged area in cold water—but not so icy that he suffers shock, of course. Rather than fill a pail or bowl, I'd suggest the sink—it's a convenient bath for a scalded under-five, and you can keep the burnt arms or whatever in it until the pain has subsided.

Remove any steaming clothes. (If you've ever plunged a rubber-gloved hand into the washing-machine only to find there's a hole in one finger, you'll know how clothes retain heat.) When the worst of the burn—and a scald is a wet burn—has gone, pat him dry and cover the injured area loosely with a clean dry bandage. If the affected area is larger than the size of his hand, it's serious; take the child to a doctor.

Also on the subject of hot water: use a large sponge for

301

bathing. Babies sometimes put small soft ones into their mouths and choke.

Another treacherous plaything, surprisingly, is his talc. Inhaled powder can obstruct the air passages. Now, if your baby's anything like mine were, he'll want to hold the talcum powder every time you use it on him. I don't see any harm in this, provided you check that the container is closed when he takes it. The important thing is not to leave him playing with the talc afterwards in his crib. He could open the container.

Need I say: never leave him alone in the bath for a second? He can drown in a few inches of water, and fast, because at this age he won't struggle.

Asphyxia

This seems a good moment to tell you about the treatment for asphyxia. It's The Kiss of Life, a dramatic name for mouth-to-mouth artificial respiration, and you should employ it at once whenever breathing has stopped. I know babies breathe so quietly that many a mother has woken her first-born just to check he's still alive! But that's usually in the dark. In daylight she should be able to see his chest moving up and down. So if you can't see any such movement and you can't hear your baby exhaling either, check his breath against a mirror: it should steam up. If it doesn't, quick—start the mouth-to-mouth resuscitation.

I hardly need add that if you rescue his limp, silent form from under water, you don't start hunting through three old handbags for a mirror to assure yourself that he isn't breathing. If he's not coughing, he's not breathing.

Place him on his back, and with one hand press his forehead down; with the other lift his chin up. This prevents his tongue from obstructing the back of the throat. Maintain this position all the time.

1. *Take a deep breath.*
2. *Open your mouth. Seal your lips round your baby's mouth and nose.*
3. *Puff air very gently but firmly into his mouth and so into his lungs.*
4. *Remove your mouth, turning your head to look at his chest, which should have risen and now be falling as the air comes out.*
5. *Repeat the cycle.*

Continue puffing at a steady rate until he can breathe for himself. At that stage, turn him on his side because he may vomit.

If, on the other hand, his skin remains blue-gray in color, the carotid pulse at the side of neck is absent, and his pupils are widely dilated, then his heart has ceased beating, too. Keep calm; there's something you can do about that as well. Officially it's called external heart compression.

First of all slap his chest smartly over the lower part of the breastbone. That in itself is often enough to start the beat. If it fails, overcome your desperation and put two

303

fingers on the lower half of the breastbone, keeping your palm off his chest. Then press the breastbone down firmly with a rocking movement fifteen times, which should take about nine seconds. Then quickly and smoothly alternate with two more inflations of the lung. Eventually you should be rewarded by both a flickery pulse and a few gasps.

If you've been trying unsuccessfully for, say, fifteen minutes, phone for an ambulance. But don't do that precipitately, because the half-minute it'll take you to dial could be fatal for your baby. Obviously, if there's someone else available, get him or her to phone at once while you get on with the treatment; afterwards that other person can do the heart-massage while you look after the breathing. It should still be an alternate treatment—heart-lung, heart-lung—but two people can make it more effective by giving one inflation of the lung to five presses on the breastbone.

Hypothermia

Now, it is just possible that in a very cold atmosphere a new baby can stop breathing. He hasn't suffocated or drowned or swallowed anything; his only symptom is that he is deathly cold to the touch. This is hypothermia—loss of body heat.

Whenever a person stops breathing, mouth-to-mouth resuscitation is your first priority. Once breathing is re-established, you should gradually raise your baby's body temperature by wrapping him in blankets and giving him warm milk to drink, providing, of course, he is conscious. Do not toss him about to get the circulation going—his little body needs all the energy it's got simply to survive.

Since mothers have become aware of the danger of hypothermia, however, there have been far more two-month-olds panting under woollies in a heat wave than fading away in some chill room. Still, it's something to bear in mind, especially for a winter baby. Ideally, his room temperature shouldn't fall below 65°. But however cold the weather may be, don't be tempted to leave a hot-water bottle or electric pad in your baby's crib with him. It's just asking for scalds and burns. Pop them in while he's out being fed, and take them out when you put him back.

Besides, if he's wearing a stretch sleeping-suit (and I approve of them wholeheartedly) he won't be quite so susceptible to cold sheets on bare legs. Another advantage of those suits is that they have no nasty little ribbons round the neck. Apart from the fact that your ingenious baby will drive you mad by pulling them out, he just might get one half-out, roll over awkwardly, and strangle himself with it.

And while we're on the subject: beware his glorious christening shawl. His fingers could become entangled in those lacy patterns and serious harm could result.

Ah yes, and although there are pretty pillow-slips in the shops with "baby" embroidered in one corner, pillows for babies are both unnecessary and dangerous, due to the risk of suffocation. When your baby is old enough to sit up in his carriage, he can have a pillow tucked behind his back for comfort. But it should be taken away whenever he lies down. If you can avoid using a pillow in his crib or bed until he is old enough to ask for one, all the better. My own children didn't ask for pillows until they were old enough to want to sit up in bed to read. The spine and back muscles grow stronger for being allowed to function correctly.

Finally, make sure his toys (or anything else you give him to play with, like a spoon) are small enough for him to hold safely, but too large to swallow. And remember that plastic breaks easily; so be on the look-out for bits that snap off.

Burns

The time between the ages of one and two is, where safety is concerned, a nightmare era. Your baby is fully mobile, but none too steady, and he wants to touch everything he sees. Burns are the worst enemy here. So let's kick off with some big dos and don'ts.

1. *Use a fixed firescreen round all fires, and designate the fireplace a prohibited area, even when it's not alight.*
2. *Keep matches away from your child. Matchboxes are small and rattly, and have instant infant appeal.*
3. *Never air diapers, or anything else, on the firescreen. They're more than likely to catch fire.*
4. *Buy flame-resistant clothes and fabrics for nightwear.*

If your toddler ever does burn himself, first put out any flames by rolling him in a blanket or coat. Then tear off smoldering clothes by seizing them in a part where they're not burning. (Otherwise there'll be two of you in the hospital.) Never prick blisters or slap on soap. Simply follow the cool-water treatment I've described for scalds. And if you're only seconds away from water, it's better not to remove clothes—because anything burnt is sterile.

Though less of a killer statistically, there are more cases of scalding than burning among small children. Most such accidents would be prevented if parents remembered:

1. *To turn pan handles out of reach. No self-respecting toddler can ignore something sticking out just above his head. He has to fetch it down and inspect . . . and that's how he gets three pints of boiling water over him.*

2. *Never to pass hot drinks over his head. It's not likely you'll spill any, but why risk it?*

3. *To keep teapots, kettles, and hot-water bottles away from the edges of counters or tables, and to tuck up the tempting overhang of a tablecloth.*

4. *To keep an eye on the cord of the electric coffee-pot. There's not much point in having the boiling water safely out of reach, if a few good pulls on the cord will bring down the pot.*

5. *To bar Baby from the kitchen when you're transferring food from oven to plates.*

6. *To teach him by example the rule "cold before hot" for washing and bathing.*

307

Fractures

The baby between one and two is in constant danger from falls. The worst trouble comes from stairs and windows. Even if he can't reach up to the windows, bear in mind that he can drag a chair across and stand on that. So play safe. Use bars. Fix a stair-gate across a flight which he may one day, without the necessary skill, decide to climb up or down.

Let's spend a moment on serious injuries. If your eighteen-month-old has a bad fall—down the cellar steps, for instance—your first impulse will be to pick him up and cuddle him. Don't—he may have broken something, in which case he should not be moved until the fracture has been strapped. Comfort him, and check for a fracture, probably a greenstick one. (Children's bones tend to break like green twigs—on the outside, with the inside remaining firm.)

If it's a limb that's hurt, get him to try and move it. If he can't, I'm afraid it probably is a fracture. A swelling round the painful area is another give-away, or if the limb appears slightly deformed. Treatment: unless you are miles from the nearest ambulance station—in which case learn in advance about bandaging fractures—I'd advise you to do nothing except dash to a telephone. That done, return to keep your patient company until the experts arrive. Make him comfortable—a cushion under his head, say, and maintain his body temperature.

I use that phrase because people are aware they must

308

"keep the patient warm" and frequently insist on bundling blankets over a fellow too hurt to protest on a steaming day. He needs a blanket or coat over him only if he's cold from shock or the weather is chill.

If your toddler appears to have no breakages (I say "appears" because it is possible that he may complain of pain a day or two later and an X-ray will reveal a crack), then attend to any minor wound. First wash your hands thoroughly. Then with a swab of sterile absorbent cotton dipped in warm soapy water, remove any loose foreign matter (glass, metal, gravel, etc.) from the wound's surface, but don't go pulling at anything that's embedded. That's a job for the doctor. Gravel out of the way, gently clean the wound with more cotton, taking care not to disturb any blood clots. Finally bandage with a prepared sterile dressing.

If the bleeding is severe and the blood seeps through the dressing, put another one on top. And in cases where no fracture is suspected, raise the injured part. Then call the doctor or an ambulance. Only an expert can say whether stitches or an anti-tetanus shot will be necessary.

I should warn you that in the event of a serious accident, you may find your child UNCONSCIOUS. Don't panic; he'll come around. But call for medical help—all cases of concussion should be seen by a doctor. And don't assume that because he's sitting up crying when you reach him, he didn't lose consciousness at all. He could have, during that moment it took you to run from the kitchen to the yard. If he can't remember actually colliding with the tree, only running toward it, then he's concussed. And even

309

if his head seems to be on straight, watch out for mysterious headaches over the next few days.

Never give a person who has been seriously injured a drink, sweet warm milk or anything else. He may need an anaesthetic, which necessitates an empty stomach for four hours beforehand. The last thing a loving mother wants to do is to delay an urgent operation, or subject her child to that medical horror: the stomach-pump.

Poisoning

The average home is full of poisons. Not 007 cyanide pills, but plain ordinary cleaning materials. For convenience we usually store these under the sink—which is right on your child's level. Put the saucepans down there instead, and move the deadly bleaches and ammonia somewhere else.

Make sure insecticides, weed killers, rat poison, etc., in the garage are not just lying about on the floor. They should be on a sturdy shelf a good five feet up, or locked away in a cupboard.

And then there are medicines—especially sugar-coated tablets. Please keep these in a medicine cabinet, and not lying around on your bedside table.

I appreciate that if your husband's got an odd pint of primrose paint on a fine Sunday morning and offers to do over Jimmy's crib, or his toy truck, the last thing you want to do is deter him. But check that the paint or varnish he intends to use is non-toxic.

310

A last comment on the subject of poisons: when your child is playing outside, look out for lethal plants, like deadly nightshade, toadstools, and laburnum. He hasn't yet outgrown the habit of putting new things in his mouth, and if the wrong thing goes in and down, he'll know it.

Or he may not. He may have taken sleeping tablets and be unconscious. Call an ambulance. With poisons that should be your first move and, if you know what your child's taken, tell the ambulance men. It could save valuable analysis time when deciding on the antidote.

Electric Shock

Beware of electric sockets. The three-year-old playing with, say, metal xylophone hammers, is in far greater danger than the baby with his tiny poking fingers. Those long sticks can be inserted in those little holes. Forbid him to touch electric sockets. But I wouldn't count absolutely on his unfailing obedience, and he need fail only once. Put blind plugs in sockets not in use, and never leave lamps about without bulbs in every socket.

If the child does somehow manage to give himself a shock, first break the contact by switching off the current or, if that is not possible, by standing on dry insulating material (rubber, thickly folded newspaper, book, wood) and using some similar insulating material to knock him clear of the contact. Don't rush up and pull him with bare hands. Electrifying yourself as well won't save him. Once he's freed, administer first aid in order of precedence: (1) breathing and heart; (2) burns; (3) shock.

Road Accidents

Talking of first-aid precedence reminds me to say that almost any road accident involving a young child is a job for the experts. Call an ambulance at once, or make sure someone else does. And I mean *make sure*. There have been tragic cases of a dozen or so witnesses to an accident, all convinced somebody else has phoned for an ambulance. But while you're waiting for the ambulance to arrive, do the following:

1. *Preserve life.*
   As I've said, this means artificial respiration and heart compression as necessary.
   Control bleeding with firm bandages and, whenever no fracture is suspected, by raising the injured part.
2. *Prevent the condition from becoming worse.*
   Cover the wound.
   Immobilize fractures.
3. *Help recovery.*
   Comfort and reassure.
   Protect him from cold.
   Stop spectators from crowding around.

But talking of road accidents is looking on the black side. I hope sincerely that they will be prevented. On the street, set your two-year-old a good example. This is far more valuable than a hundred lectures and warnings. And when you're on a busy street, you may find walking-reins more comfortable than clutching a tiny paw. You should do one or the other. Of course, if you have a baby in a carriage as well, and something to carry in your left hand, you are excused. Under these circumstances train your youngster to hold on to the carriage.

Drowning

For the three-and-a-half to five year old, drowning is among the greatest hazards. I realize that four-year-olds want to explore beyond the confines of their own backyards, but never let your child play by water unsupervised.

The same holds true, of course, when wet patches are iced over, and tempting to slide on. Unless there has been a long cold spell, the ice may be too thin to maintain even the weight of a child. Treacherously, it sometimes will hold just long enough for him to reach the middle.

Just one thing to say about bathing at the seashore, besides the obvious one of not going near the water when no lifeguard is on duty. It has to do with floating rubber mattresses. They're fun, and may help your child conquer any fear of the water. But don't let him lie on one when you're not right next to him. They can drift out to sea fast, especially on an outgoing tide.

313

Finally, if you are sailing or boating with a young child, see that he wears a life jacket that fits.

In the event of drowning, The Kiss of Life is slightly different for an older child. You seal your lips round his mouth only, and pinch his nostrils shut with the fingers of one hand, making sure you keep his head well back. And although you blow gently, it'll need to be a little stronger than the puff you'd use for a baby. This time the heart massage is done with the heel of your free hand, and the rocking is slower, only a little more than one rock per second.

Odds and Ends

In the last decade a frightening new killer has emerged on our domestic scene—the plastic bag. The ghastly part about it is it's so *useful:* ideal for transporting wet diapers, for keeping woollies clean, for putting food in. But *never, never* let your child get hold of one. He can suffocate in seconds if he puts one over his head. (See treatment for asphyxia.) Despite the bags' waterproof quality, don't be tempted to use one as an undersheet; even a fragment can catch in the throat and obstruct the air passages.

For safety in a car, what your child really needs is an approved car-seat. I know they're pretty expensive but they're the only totally secure method for him to travel in a car. What's more: they're often designed so that they raise

314

their small passenger to window-level, and to have a child who enjoys the car because he can see out is a wonderful convenience.

I think I should recap here something I said about teaching your young child to cope with his environment, dangers and all. It's much more valuable to show your child how to use scissors, knives, and hammers (in safe, simplified versions) than to keep these tools forever out of his reach. Don't forget, too, that often simple curiosity drives under-fives to grab the bread knife and examine it. If they've never been told what it's for and warned, "Bread knives have to be very sharp so that we can cut bread with them, that's why we're always careful with them"—who can guess what they might do to themselves?

However, once again gradual introduction is the operative phrase. Even at three-and-a-half there are many tools too dangerous for him to have access to. A sharpened lawn-mower, for instance, should be shut away at all times; so should razor blades and the carving knife.

As you are aware, I'm against frustrating children by *forbidding* them to jump or climb. But you can help your child to become proficient in these skills and thus avoid some of those harder falls. Far better for you and him to have a quiet exploratory try-out of the climbing apparatus in the yard or playground, than for his first experience with it to be chasing an older child to the top!

Minor tumbles can often be avoided just by doing up a shoelace or strap. Your child may not yet be able to deal with a flapping lace himself but, if instructed, he can approach an adult for assistance.

315

The Medicine Chest

With all the knocks and cuts and bruises your child is going to receive, I think it might be helpful if I gave you a basic medicine chest.

Plain white gauze in half-yard packages	*These are for minor cuts, which should be washed with soap and water before bandaging.*
Assorted roller bandages	
Assorted adhesive dressings	
Adhesive tape	
Plastic bowl	*Apparatus for above.*
Sterile absorbent cotton	
Assorted sizes of prepared sterile dressings	*For bandaging wounds.*
Cheesecloth	*To be soaked in cold water for use on bruises—before they swell.*
Small package of tissues	*For wiping away mud, etc.*
Safety-pins	*Sometimes easier than tying a bandage.*
Scissors	*For cutting the bandages.*

316

Antihistamine cream	*For treating insect bites and stings. (First remove the sting, if present. In the event of a sting in the mouth, take the child to the hospital.)*
Calamine lotion	*For treating sunburn.*
Clinical thermometer	*For taking temperature.*

In conclusion I should point out that I have only been able to discuss very general safety problems, and I've covered only basic first aid. If you want to learn more, and everyone should, get in touch with your local branch of the Red Cross.

38

Off to School

When your child reaches the end of the age-span of this book—in other words five—he will be a year away from first grade. Emotionally, socially, educationally, this will be a vast step away from being at home all day with you, playing with whichever toy suits his fancy at any particular moment. So, in accordance with the gradual approach I have advocated in everything pertaining to children, I believe your child should attend nursery school before he is five and kindergarten when he reaches five.

The Value of the Preschool Experience

Preschool education will afford him the opportunity of coping without you on a regular basis—anything from a couple of mornings a week to five full schooldays. So when the inevitable 9 o'clock till 3:15 parting arrives, it won't be a painful wrench.

At grade school, too, your child will be expected to be respectful to (but certainly not terrified of) a teacher, and he will be expected to work in a class full of other children. That's a bit different from being polite to the friend who drops in, or playing contentedly for an hour with the little girl next door. Preschool education helps to prepare your child for dealing with so many individuals.

Finally, preschool education is invaluable in teaching your child *how to learn*. At school, the pupil who wants to know is the pupil who gets ahead. Nursery school and kindergarten will stimulate his mind in a way that encourages him to want to find out.

Throughout this book I have spoken of your child's need for companionship, and increasingly the companionship of his contemporaries. And I have spoken of his need for a "child-oriented environment"—a place where everything exists for the purpose of the child, where the only "nos" are acts that are strictly anti-social, like hitting your "friend" on the head.

When Should He Go?

So when is your child ready for nursery school? Well, *they* won't take him before he's two and out of diapers, and many schools will not take him until he's three.

Now, while I believe all children should be encouraged to play with their contemporaries, I am not going to be so foolish as to state that at some arbitrary age each one is ready to go off to nursery school each morning. In this, as in everything, your child is an individual. Some children, despite having gradually been weaned away from you with sitters, are not ready for this break as early as others. Some, like my son, are ready to go off at fourteen months!

When Nicholas was that age, Merle was going to nursery school and Tina to grade school, and both sisters obviously looked forward to rushing off to this thing called school. Nicholas's great cry of frustration every morning as he sat in his high chair finishing his toast and watching them gaily leaving was: "Chool!" I told him that fourteen months was too young for school, but it still took me most of the rest of the morning to get him to play contentedly at home.

Then, when he was almost sixteen months old, I took the bull by the horns and went along to the nursery school where his sister was going, and I told the teacher my problem. "I have a sixteen-month-old child who wants to come to nursery school. What shall I do?"

And she said, "Oh dear . . . well, you know I can't take him." But I still stood there, and she thought about it. Being a very understanding person who knew about chil-

320

dren, she said: "Tell me: can he eat entirely independently?"

And I said: "Almost."

"Can he walk entirely on his own?"

"Nearly."

"Good. When he can eat by himself, when he can walk, and when he's potty-trained, bring him to me."

So when Nicholas was eighteen months old he went to nursery school every day, and attended full-time because he was so happy there that he refused to go home at lunchtime.

But he was exceptional, and so was that nursery school teacher. As a general rule, I would say that eighteen months is the time to find out what is available for your child in your area, and at what age they will admit him. But don't take anyone's word about whether a particular nursery school is good or bad. Read up about the various approaches to nursery education.

Private nursery schools use various methods—for instance, the permissive Froebel approach or the much more disciplined Montessori approach. "Disciplined" does not mean that the children sit at tiny desks facing the blackboard while the teacher talks. But exponents of the Montessori system will agree, I am sure, that their handling of education follows a more formal pattern. Decide what you want before choosing a school.

321

Goodbye, Baby

And when your child does start going off each day, you will feel—as all mothers do—a little sad that your "baby" is growing up. But don't be sad. Be proud—your child has taken his first big step on the road to maturity.

Index

Index

329